WINNING **BIG** IN
COLORADO SMALL CLAIMS COURT

How to Sue and Collect
2nd Edition

Charles P. Brackney, Esq.

 BRADFORD PUBLISHING COMPANY

PLEASE READ

This book, *Winning Big in Small Claims Court: How to Sue and Collect*, 2nd edition, is intended to provide general information with regard to the subject matter covered. It is not meant to provide legal opinions or offer advice, nor to serve as a substitute for advice by licensed, legal professionals. It is sold with the understanding that Bradford Publishing Company is not engaged in rendering legal or other professional services.

Bradford Publishing Company and the author do not warrant that the information herein is complete or accurate, and do not assume and hereby disclaim any liability to any person for any loss or damage caused by errors, inaccuracies or omissions, or usage of this book or its forms.

Laws, and interpretations of those laws, change frequently and the subject matter of this book contains important legal consequences. It is the responsibility of the user of this book to know if the information contained in it are applicable to his or her situation, and if necessary, to consult legal, tax or other counsel.

Publisher's Cataloging-in-Publication
(Provided by Quality Books, Inc.)

Brackney, Charles P.
   Winning big in Colorado small claims court: how to
sue and collect / Charles P. Brackney. -- 2nd ed.
   p. cm.
   Includes index.
   ISBN 1-883726-75-1

   1. Small claims court--Colorado.   2. Title

KFC2321.B73 2002   347.788'04
                                      QBI02-200288

Winning Big in Small Claims Court:
How to Sue and Collect
ISBN: 1-883726-75-1

This book is dedicated to my wife, Deborah Brackney.
Her unwavering support for me is just one reason I love her.

ACKNOWLEDGMENTS

The author would like to thank the following people: Jerry Klein for his help with the title; Alan Hutchins for answering my questions about the insurance industry; Don Harder for the insights from his experiences in Small Claims Court; and Lucinda Miller for steering me in the right direction.

Table of Contents

Chapter 1: An Introduction to Small Claims Court

IS SMALL CLAIMS COURT FOR YOU?

Your landlord won't return your deposit after you've moved out of your old apartment. Your car has suffered minor damage in an accident. You paid a business to perform a service and now they refuse to do it. Your next-door neighbor knocked down part of your privacy fence when he put in a backyard basketball court.

In each of these situations, you have suffered a financial loss because of the actions or inactions of someone else. Fairness would dictate that you be compensated. However, you may be tempted to just forget about pursuing the matter because the amount of money involved isn't that much. While you wouldn't hesitate to seek the services of an attorney if you had suffered damages totaling $100,000, it may be that you couldn't even cover the legal fees in a case where "only" $1,000 is at stake—and that's if you're lucky enough to collect. You're not happy about it, but going any farther seems like too much trouble.

You've considered the idea of taking your case to Small Claims Court, but are wary of the obstacles to success. You know what happened in your case and why you deserve to be compensated. You can easily explain to your spouse, your friends, and your family how you were wronged and why some-

1

one should pay you money to make up for it. What seems daunting is the prospect of having to explain it to a judge you've never met in front of a roomful of strangers. Also intimidating you is the need to get all the paperwork straight while navigating through the unfamiliar world of the legal system, with its plaintiffs, defendants, bailiffs, impossible to understand rules and strange terminology. Finally, you may be skeptical that you can prevail over an affluent individual or a large association or business. It's easy just to write off the experience as a lesson learned and move on.

People just like you win cases everyday in small claims courts all across Colorado. They believe their claims to compensation are worth pursuing, not abandoning, even if the amount is not enough to justify hiring a lawyer. They've familiarized themselves with the rules and procedures of Small Claims Court, and have done the preparation necessary to bring a successful action. They've done this on their own, without the aid of an attorney. You can, too.

WHAT IS SMALL CLAIMS COURT?

The Colorado General Assembly enacted legislation in 1976 creating a small claims division in each County Court in the state. The legislature did this because it was concerned that individuals, associations, and even small businesses frequently did not pursue valid small claims in civil cases because of the expense of retaining legal counsel and the time and effort such litigation usually required. They also realized that the intricacies of the law and the complicated rules of court procedure deterred many who had legitimate claims to compensation. They sought to create a forum where claims involving a relatively small amount of money could be resolved in an inexpensive, speedy, and informal manner. While the substantive law still governs in Small Claims Court, many of the technical rules of pleading and evidence have been relaxed to make the process friendlier to people bringing actions without an attorney. Finally, the legislature deemed that small claims cases should be heard at times convenient for Colorado citizens, including evenings and Saturdays, and that court personnel in the small claims divisions be trained to assist anyone interested in utilizing the small claims process.

The experiment in making the courts more accessible to the average citizen has proven successful, both in Colorado and elsewhere. Every state now has some variation of the small claims court concept. Since the establishment of small claims courts in Colorado in the late 1970's, thousands of such cases have been filed. Figures for the most recent twelve-month period show that Colorado Small Claims Courts now handle over 20,000 cases per year. Remember that each one of these filings represents someone who was willing to enter the legal system without the benefit of legal counsel.

In addition to reducing complexity and expense, Small Claims Court can provide you with another advantage over the more traditional legal system—time. Again, the whole idea behind Small Claims Court is to provide citizens with a place for the easy and quick resolution of disputes. Cases brought in Small Claims Court are often decided within a month of the initial filing. Compare this with the months or even years a case may be in litigation in a County or District Court. By removing many of the complicated rules and procedures of the regular court process and eliminating attorneys altogether, cases are more likely to be focused on the central dispute, thus simplifying them and allowing for a more speedy resolution. To read the actual laws and rules of Small Claims Court, see Appendix D in this book.

The establishment of small claims courts has allowed many citizens to bring disputes to court which otherwise may have been unresolved. This lack of a resolution often allowed one party to benefit unfairly at the expense of another because the former knew it was unlikely that an expensive and time-consuming action would be brought by the latter when only a small amount of money was at stake.

Let's look now at some of the more typical situations seen in Small Claims Court.

COMMON CASE SCENARIOS IN SMALL CLAIMS COURTS

The laws and rules pertaining to Small Claims Court spell out certain requirements that must be met before a case is eligible to be heard as a small claim. However, with only a few exceptions, the laws and rules do not limit the type of case which can be brought in Small Claims Court. Again, the intent of the Colorado legislature in establishing the Small Claims Court was to make it as accessible to as many people in as many situations as possible. Do not think that just because the case you are considering filing in Small Claims Court is unusual that it is not appropriate for resolution in this forum. Given that Small Claims Courts have heard thousands and thousands of cases over the years, chances are, no matter how strange your case may seem, a small claims judge has seen it already!

There are, however, certain types of case situations which are the most likely to turn up in Small Claims Court. Here are some of the most common examples:

- A customer suing a business to return a deposit for goods never delivered or services never performed.
- A driver suing another driver for damages caused to the former's automobile.
- A small business seeking to recover from someone who has written a bad check to pay for goods or services.
- An employee of a small business who was paid with a bad check.
- A loan which the other party refuses to repay.
- A customer suing a dry cleaning business because an article of clothing was lost or damaged.
- A tenant suing a landlord for refusing to return a security deposit.
- A landlord suing a tenant for damages to an apartment.
- A car owner suing a garage for faulty motor vehicle repair.

Even though these cases are among those which are most frequently brought in Small Claims Court, they still must meet the basic rules, such as timing and dollar amount limits, that any small claim must abide by and which will be discussed in more detail later.

The general rule is that only cases in which you are seeking money from another party can be brought in Small Claims Court. You cannot get divorced in Small Claims Court, you cannot evict someone from an apartment, you cannot change your name, you cannot sue for libel or slander, you cannot sue your employer for wrongful discharge, nor can you get an injunction or restraining order. You cannot bring a class action suit in Small Claims Court, but an organization of people such as a homeowner's association could sue as a group. There are a few exceptions: you can sue to be released from a contract or to enforce the terms of a contact. You can sue to seek the return of personal property. You may also seek to enforce restrictive covenants on residential real estate. However, these are clearly defined exceptions to the general rule.

The main point to bear in mind here is that there are very few limits on the types of cases that can be brought in Small Claims Court. Just because a certain situation doesn't appear on the list of typical small claims cases above does not mean it is inappropriate for Small Claims Court. Your case may very well be ideal for Small Claims Court.

CAN YOU REALLY WIN A CASE WITHOUT AN ATTORNEY?

There is no requirement in any case in any court in Colorado that a party initiating or defending against a legal action be represented by legal counsel. However, with the increasingly complex nature of both the law itself and the accompanying court process, very few average citizens feel comfortable pursuing a case in either District Court or County Court without the assistance of an attorney.

But Small Claims Court is different. It is designed for the person who wants to pursue a case without an attorney. In fact, parties are not allowed to have legal representation in small claims cases. People bringing cases in Small Claims Court need not be legally trained, have any prior experience with the court system, or be familiar with the rules governing lawyers and the practice of law. Rather, they need to know only a few basic rules of procedure, and be able to present the facts in their case to the court in a clear and concise manner.

This is not to say that successfully pursuing a case in Small Claims Court is easy. There are two key elements you must remember if you wish to take full advantage of what Small Claims Court offers the non-attorney litigant: preparation and perseverance. While it is clearly easier on your wallet to not have to hire an attorney to prosecute your case, not having one working for you means that you will have to do the legwork necessary to convince the court that someone else has damaged you and owes you money. The full burden of preparing the case falls on you.

Second, you must be prepared to stick with the case. The system is intentionally set up to be debtor-friendly, often making collection of a judgment very difficult. Many debtors are in bankruptcy, are chronically unemployed, or live only on the proceeds of Social Security or Workers' Compensation. These situations further decrease your chances of collection. Because your ultimate goal is not just to prevail in Small Claims Court but, rather, to collect money, you must not give up in your attempts to collect what is rightfully due you. Perseverance is a must in a small claims action.

"Winning big" in Small Claims Court does not necessarily mean obtaining a judgment for a large amount of money. Rather, the concept of winning big has more to do with the importance your claim has to you. In your mind, your case is the most important one the court has to consider. By becoming familiar with the workings of Small Claims Court, the strategies you can use in your case, and the best ways to collect the money you are due, you can greatly increase your odds of success in a small claims case. The advantage you will have over other parties in Small Claims Court will be considerable. The background and knowledge this book provides may be the difference between success and failure in your case – the biggest case of all.

The goal of this book is to provide you with the tools and knowledge you will need to pursue your case in Small Claims Court successfully. It walks you step-by-step through the rules, forms, and procedures you need to be aware of as you proceed through the unfamiliar legal system. The appendices at the end of this book contain additional information about the laws of Colorado, forms you will need and a checklist you can use to make sure you've covered all the important points in your case. With adequate preparation and perseverance, YOU CAN WIN IN SMALL CLAIMS COURT.

Chapter 2: Determining if Your Case is Right for Small Claims Court

WHO IS LIABLE?

You're interested in taking a case to Small Claims Court because you have been damaged or have suffered some form of financial loss. You're confident that you can prove this to the court because you can provide a copy of a bad check you were given, a contract whose terms were unfulfilled, or witnesses who will testify that your property has suffered damage. Surely a judge will agree that you're entitled to compensation.

However, proving convincingly that you've been damaged is not enough. You must also prove that the party you're seeking money from is legally liable to you for the damage or other loss. Oftentimes this is an indisputable matter. If someone gives you a bad check in return for goods or services you provided, the maker of that check is clearly liable to you for the amount of that check. If a driver of a car runs into your fence, odds are you have a case for damages against that person.

But, in other instances, you must check to be sure that there is some legal basis for your claim. This often means proving the existence of a legal contract between you and the other party. This is most easily done when there is a written agreement between you and that party. A contract need not be in writing to be valid and legally enforceable. The key point is whether a binding agreement, either written or verbal, was ever reached.

Let's say you offer to mow your neighbor's lawn tomorrow. Your neighbor says yes, she would like you to mow her lawn tomorrow. The next day, you do cut the neighbor's grass, but when you knock on her door to collect payment for your hard work, she says she isn't going to pay you because she didn't really "mean it," and, besides, the two of you never agreed on a price.

What she doesn't seem to realize is that her reply to you the day before, which you reasonably took to be an agreement for you to mow her lawn, is sufficient to create a perfectly valid contract. You have lived up to your end of the bargain by cutting the grass, and she must now live up to hers by paying you. The fact that there was no prior discussion of the price is not critical. A court would rule that you are due a reasonable price for your labor even if you had not set out the exact dollar amount in advance.

This result would not occur if her reply to your offer of lawn mowing services had been "that's an interesting idea. I'll think about it." In that situation, you would not be able to collect from her had you gone ahead and mowed the grass the next day. This is because there was no point in time at which an agreement between you and your neighbor was in place, so no legally enforceable contract was ever created. Simply stated, there is no liability, contractual or otherwise, which would extend to your neighbor in this case.

Confusion can also arise in cases where there is a written agreement. Be sure that your claim involves something that is expressly provided for in the contract. The damages that are easiest to prove arise out of a failure to deliver a specific good or service contained in such an agreement. Also be watchful for warranty clauses. If a local nursery plants lilac bushes in your backyard and promises in writing that they will replace any that die within one year of planting, you may not recover if one starts wilting after eighteen months.

Parents can sometimes be held liable for the damage caused by their minor children who live with them. Such liability can be transferred to the parents when a minor maliciously or willfully damages or destroys property, or knowingly causes bodily injury. The maximum amount of damages that may be collected from the parents is $3,500. Parents may also be held liable when a minor child steals merchandise from a store. The penalty in these situations is the amount of actual damage based on the stolen items, plus an additional $100 to $250 dollars, as determined by the court.

NEGLIGENCE

Liability can also be an issue in cases involving negligence. Consider the person who attends a Rockies game and parks his car at a private parking lot near Coors Field. After the game, he returns to find that his vehicle has been broken into and his personal property is missing. He may be tempted to say that the operators of the parking lot should pay him for his losses because their lot was not patrolled. If the lot never claimed to be secure, which means the operator never made any promise, express or implied, to the car owner that his car would be safe, the lot operators are not liable. However, this result might be different if the parking lot had advertised monitored parking in a secure facility. Then the lot operators could be held liable because of their negligence.

Negligence is defined as the failure to exercise, in a given situation, the degree of care which a reasonable person would use in the same circumstances. Failure to be reasonable in that situation is negligent behavior. This reasonableness standard can arise out of either an action which a reasonable person would not have taken in a given circumstance or out of an inaction or failure to perform an act whose commission would be necessary to meet the minimum threshold of reasonableness based on a duty to act.

Confused? Determining what is the exact level of care required in a specific situation is not always easy. First let's consider some of the more obvious examples. Say an inattentive driver hits you from behind while you are stopped at a red light. This driver did not meet the standard of care called for in that situation, namely avoiding collisions with other cars, property and pedestrians. This driver was negligent and is therefore liable to you for the damage to your car. The same would be true if this driver was not paying attention and, as a result, that driver's car jumped onto the curb and smashed into the fence surrounding your property.

There are also examples of negligent behavior based on inaction. Perhaps a person with a malfunctioning washing machine calls a repairman and tells him that the machine's motor is not operating and that there have been water leaks from some of the hose connections. The repairman says he'll "take care of it." However, he gets very involved in fixing the problem with the motor, and does not bother to check on the hoses, one of which comes loose the next week during the rinse cycle, spilling water everywhere and causing considerable damage. Under these circumstances, the repairman had a duty to check and repair the hoses. Because he acted unreasonably in not doing so, he acted negligently and is liable to the washing machine owner for the damage.

Many situations, however, are not so clear-cut. If a strong wind knocks over a tree in your neighbor's yard and onto your porch, could your neighbor be considered negligent? Did the neighbor exercise reasonable care regarding the planting and care of the tree? Should the neighbor have had the tree removed because it was old and ready to fall over when the next stiff breeze arose? These types of situations are often decided on a case-by-case basis, depending on the specific facts of each case.

The key concept is reasonableness. The more it feels to you that the other party was unreasonable, the better case you probably have. If you can say that the other party's lack of reasonable conduct led to your financial injury, you may have a claim based on negligence.

RESCISSION OF A CONTRACT

You may also sue in Small Claims Court to be let out of the obligations of a contract. This is known as "rescission." The notion behind the concept of rescission is to put both parties back to where they were before the contract was signed. This remedy is appropriate in situations in which you have signed an agreement to pay for merchandise or a service, but the other party has failed to come through. You may sue to ask that the contract be invalidated and for the return of any money you have paid the other party to that point. You can also seek rescission as a defendant if the other party sues you for not paying for the goods or services as provided for in the contract.

A determination of who is liable to you for your damage

or loss may not always be as difficult as in these situations, but it is nonetheless an essential first step in deciding how to proceed after you've suffered a loss. The next is to determine the extent of your financial loss.

SPECIFIC PERFORMANCE OF A CONTRACT

You may bring a case in Small Claims Court to seek specific performance with the terms of a contract. This means you, as the plaintiff, may ask the court to order the other party to a contract, who would become the defendant, to comply with the terms of that contract. This may or may not involve the payment of a monetary settlement. However, the amount at issue or the act you seek to have the other party perform must not exceed the standard jurisdictional limit of $7,500.

RETURN OF PERSONAL PROPERTY

Small Claims Court also provides you with a mechanism for compelling another party to return to you personal property belonging to you that is in the possession of the other party who refuses to return it. The law uses the term "replevin" to describe this kind of case. You can ask the Small Claims Court to require a defendant to return specific goods to you. The defendant is then deprived of the use of your property until the case is resolved. This can make the defendant more likely to settle with you. Again, the value of the property in question cannot exceed $7,500.

HOW TO CALCULATE THE DOLLAR AMOUNT OF DAMAGES AND LOSSES

In many cases brought before the Small Claims Court, the determination of the amount of the claim is a relatively straight-forward process. You were due to receive $500 from someone who had promised you that amount in return for a service you performed, and now the other party will not pay. You are entitled to $500, plus the costs associated with bringing the action in Small Claims Court (costs will be discussed in detail in Chapter 4). Let's examine some situations where the calculation of the claim amount can be a bit trickier.

The first rule to remember is that you are not entitled to sue for the entire amount of, say, an unpaid bill if the other party has partially reimbursed you. For example, if the original contract between you and another was for $500, and you have already received a payment of $200, your claim, not counting costs, will be $300. A landlord seeking to sue a former tenant for damage the latter caused to an apartment would base the claim on the actual damage less the amount of the tenant's deposit kept by the landlord. Always remember to begin with this "net" amount.

If you have received a check in payment for money owed you, but the check is returned because there are not sufficient funds in the other party's account, Colorado law may let you seek additional compensation beyond the face value of the check. You may have seen signs in stores indicating that customers who pay with bad checks will be pursued for three times the amount of the check. This remedy is available to stores and other businesses and to any individual who has received a bad check. You can sue for triple the amount of the check, or a minimum of $100. If the check was for $300, you may claim $900. If it was for $30, you may sue for $100. Again, these amounts can be increased by the costs associated with pursuing the legal action.

There are, however, certain notice requirements you must follow before you can seek triple damages in a bad check case. You must serve a written notice on the check writer, via personal service or certified mail, which states that the check was not paid upon deposit in the bank—upon "presentment" is the legal terminology—and that he or she now has fifteen days to pay you the full amount. The notice must also state the date of the check, the name of the bank on which the check was drawn, your name, and the amount of the check. If you serve such a notice and do not receive payment in fifteen days, you may then seek triple damages.

Tenants having trouble getting back a security deposit from a landlord may also seek triple damages. You must notify the landlord of your intention to sue at least seven days prior to filing a case. This notice is best given in writing. You can then sue for three times the amount of the portion of the deposit which has been wrongfully withheld.

Triple damages are also available to customers of motor vehicle repair garages which fail to provide written or verbal estimates of repair charges, unless the customer has waived the right to such an estimate. Again, you must demand a refund from the garage before filing suit for triple damages. The demand must precede the action by 10 days, excluding Saturdays, Sundays, and legal holidays.

Employers who have failed to pay you wages without legal justification can also be sued for extra damages. You may be entitled to the amount of wages due, plus a penalty equal to either 50 percent of the wages due or the amount of wages payable to you for ten working days, whichever is greater. To seek this penalty in court, you must demand payment in writing from the employer within 60 days of the date the wages were due you.

Should your case involve damage to your property, you must determine exactly how much damage you have sustained before you can sue in Small Claims Court. Usually, you are entitled to the amount that it would take to repair the item in question. The exception to this rule is that you cannot claim an amount greater than the value of the damaged item. While $2,000 in damages to your new $19,000 automobile entitles you to sue for $2,000, the same amount in damages to your old car worth $1,500 limits your claim to $1,500. This amount, after all, is really what you have been damaged.

In determining the relevant values in property damage cases, the key concept is reasonableness. If your fence has been damaged, you should get three repair estimates from qualified firms and sue for the amount of the lowest. The same notion goes for calculating the value of your damaged property. While it is usually reasonable to give yourself the benefit of the doubt, don't try to claim your fence was brand new when it was really seven years old. You should also save any documents—bills, appraisals, receipts, written estimates— which tend to support your position regarding the value of the property damaged as well as the amount necessary to repair it. These are exactly the types of items a Small Claims Court judge will want to see when your case reaches court. If you don't have an appraisal or receipt, you can still prove the worth of the item. The true value of a car, for instance, can be estimated based on the prices found in the used car bluebook, classified ads, and with values set by insurance companies.

Some smaller personal injury cases can end up in Small Claims Court. To determine the amount you can sue for in such cases, first add the amount of any actual payments to doctors, hospitals, ambulance services, pharmacies, and any other health care providers that resulted from the injury. Next add in the amount of any lost wages you suffered as a result of the injury and its accompanying treatment, as well as any property which may have been damaged. Finally, you may claim the value of pain and suffering, which is very difficult to calculate but which you may want to ask for because, at worst, it can only be thrown out by the judge. If you don't ask for it, you definitely won't get it. While there is no precise formula for determining dollar amounts for pain and suffering from an injury, many attorneys use an amount equal to three times the total of all the medical bills stemming from the injury as a starting point. The total of these amounts should be the amount of your claim.

Generally, you are not allowed to seek punitive damages in Small Claims Court. Higher courts sometimes award punitive damages to the prevailing party over and above the amount of actual damages that party has suffered. This additional amount is meant to punish the losing party and to deter others from similar behavior. In Small Claims Court, however, you may only seek money beyond your actual damages in cases where the law specifically provides for a special penalty, such as in cases involving bad checks, security deposits, unpaid wages, and motor vehicle repairs, as discussed earlier.

THE SMALL CLAIMS COURT DOLLAR AMOUNT LIMIT: WHAT "SMALL CLAIM?!"

Because the majority of cases brought in Small Claims Court involve suits to recover money, the law governing these courts expressly sets out how much a "small claim" can be. This is known as the dollar jurisdictional limit, which is to say that the jurisdiction of the Small Claims Court extends only to cases involving claims which fall below a certain dollar amount. Claims exceeding this amount, by definition, are not "small claims" and must be heard in County Court or District Court.

The amount of money that one person considers to be a great sum may seem trifling to someone who is much more affluent. The determination of what constitutes a small claim is, by its very nature, open to many interpretations. It is the state legislature's task to decide what the proper amount should be, and even its members can't seem to make up their minds.

When the Small Claims Court was first established in Colorado in the mid-1970's, the maximum amount a person could sue for in that forum was $2,000. It was later raised to $3,500, then $5,000. Legislation effective on September 1, 2001, raised the maximum amount to $7,500. However, despite what the legislature thinks, it's probably safe to say that most citizens would not consider a loss of $7,500 to be in any way small.

The good news in all of this is that the new $7,500 jurisdictional limit increases the number of situations in which people can take advantage of the easier, cheaper, and faster forum. More people can avoid filing in County Court, with its more formal and complicated rules and (usually) more lawyers. We can expect more cases than ever to be filed in Small Claims Court.

Most cases in Small Claims Court do not involve complex determinations as to whether they fit within the $7,500 limit. If the amount being sought is $7,500 or less, it can be heard in Small Claims Court. If the amount of the claim exceeds this amount, it must be pursued elsewhere. There are, however, a few wrinkles on this simple rule you should be aware of.

When the law says that a claim may not exceed $7,500, it means you cannot ask for more than that amount in a single court action. You can still file in Small Claims Court if your claim exceeds this amount—but you will forever forfeit your claim to the amount over $7,500. In some situations, this may be the best way to go. Say you have a valid claim based on a bad check written to you in the amount of $7,700. You may decide that the advantages of Small Claims Court—faster resolution, no lawyer expense—outweigh the loss of $200. You might not even be able to retain a lawyer to take your case for $200. You can still sue in Small Claims Court and be awarded a judgment for $7,500, the lion's share of your claim. Of course, this option is far less attractive if you are owed $9,700.

After reading the scenario above, you might think it would be easy enough to file one claim for $7,500 and another for $200, thus sneaking in under the dollar amount limit while still claiming the entire amount owed. However, the rules of Small Claims Court do not allow this. Only one action may be brought for each claim. You can try to split your claims so that you can file more than one case. To do this, you will need to show that each claim is based on a separate transaction, contract, or performance of a service. Courts will consider these on a case-by-case basis, and will accept separate claims if they feel all claims are appropriate. If you can genuinely distinguish your claims and can in so doing avoid brushing up against the dollar amount limit, you should go ahead and file more than one case.

SAM'S CASE

Sam Grant owns and operates a small landscaping business out of his home. The business, Sam's Landscape Designs, is set up as a sole proprietorship. He specializes in small residential and commercial landscaping projects, done at an affordable price. His business is successful, and he seldom has any problem getting paid.

Recently, however, Sam has encountered a situation in which he has not been successful in collecting the payment on a job. Sam's neighbor, Billy T., mentioned to Sam that he knew of a person at his office, Bob Lee, who was interested in having some trees planted in his yard. Sam, who gets much of his business from such referrals, immediately called Bob Lee and scheduled an appointment.

Sam met with Bob and offered to plant four 5 foot Colorado Blue Spruce trees in Bob's backyard for $2,000. Bob agreed to this proposition, saying Sam's price was much better than he'd been quoted elsewhere. Bob wrote Sam a check for $1,000 as a 50% deposit on the work. Sam agreed to complete the job in the next two weeks.

Sam deposited Bob's check and waited for it to clear. It did, and when Sam was assured of having the funds, he purchased the trees from a local nursery, took them to Bob's house and planted them. Because it was a weekday and Bob was away at work, Sam left an envelope containing an invoice for the balance of the cost, $1,000, in Bob's mailbox. The invoice stated that payment was due within two weeks of the completion of the work.

Three weeks after planting the trees, Sam had still not heard from Bob. Sam phoned him to ask about the payment. Bob replied that he was sorry, but he had had some investments go bad in the past month, and said he didn't have any money to pay Sam, and that he could barely come up with the money to make the monthly mortgage payment on his house. Bob concluded the conversation by again apologizing to Sam, and saying he wasn't sure when he would be able to pay Sam, but that it probably would not be soon.

Sam hung up the phone worried that he was now out $1,000.

WHO CAN SUE AND BE SUED?

There are specific rules in the law of Small Claims Court which set out who can initiate and defend against an action in that forum. The general rule is that any person may sue any other person. Corporations, partnerships, associations, and other organizations may also bring actions or defend against them.

In general, you are allowed to bring actions against state and local governmental entities in Small Claims Court. These agencies can include the State of Colorado, counties, cities, and special districts. Suits against the federal government may not be brought in Small Claims Court.

The rules also discuss who shall actually represent each of these players in court.

- An individual is to represent himself or herself.
- A partnership is to be represented by an active general partner or an authorized full-time employee, a union by an authorized member or a full-time employee.
- An association or other kind of organization shall be represented by an active member or full-time employee.
- For-profit corporations can be represented by a full-time officer or a full-time employee.
- Limited Liability Companies or Partnerships can be represented by a full-time officer or active general partner.
- Nonprofit corporations may be represented by an employee or an officer who is not an attorney.
- Landlords may be represented by local property managers.

There are also special rules concerning the role of attorneys in Small Claims Court. The point, after all, is to afford parties an opportunity to present their cases on their own in a less formal atmosphere, and allowing attorney representation would change the whole nature of the proceedings. However, any of the general partners, full-time officers or employees, or active members of corporations, associations, unions, or other organizations as listed in the previous paragraph who happen to be attorneys are allowed to appear on behalf of those entities in Small Claims Court.

What if you want to sue an attorney who paid your small business with a bad check? What if an attorney, acting on his own, wants to sue you in Small Claims Court? Attorneys are allowed to represent themselves as individuals in Small Claims Court in much the same way any other citizen can. If a party to a case happens to be an attorney, the case can still be heard in Small Claims Court. The attorney is merely banned from representing others. However, should an opposing party be someone who is an attorney, you may then also be represented by an attorney, even in Small Claims Court. Finally, you should also be aware that it is permissible for a party to seek the advice of an attorney before and during the course of a small claims case.

Another result of the rule in Small Claims Court that individuals or entities must represent themselves is that collection agencies or other agents acting on behalf of someone else may not file small claims actions. Only a person or entity who is the real party to the case may bring an action in Small Claims Court.

Suits may be brought against active duty members of the military. However, federal and state law protect soldiers and sailors against default judgments, because these could be entered when military service required the other party to be absent when a case was heard. If you sue an active duty member of the armed forces, and he or she is successfully served and appears at the hearing, the case will proceed normally. However, no judgment will be granted if the other party is in the military but does not appear for the hearing. The court may appoint an attorney to represent the interests of a military defendant. Note that "active military duty" does not cover those in the reserves.

Unemancipated minors may not sue or be sued in Small Claims Court. A suit brought by a minor or against one must actually be done for or against the minor's parent or legal guardian. Keep in mind that collecting money from a minor will be a difficult task.

STATUTES OF LIMITATIONS

Another requirement for initiating any kind of legal action, including one in Small Claims Court, is that it be brought in a timely manner. The law establishes a certain time period within which an action in a given situation must be filed. This time limit, called the statute of limitations, is in place because of the concept that disputes are best settled as quickly as possible. Cases brought beyond the time limit set forth in the statute of limitations are thought to suffer from problems with stale evidence and the receding memories of witnesses. Therefore, in the interest of justice and to better allow the system to reach the correct result, many types of actions are governed by a statute of limitations.

While the effect of the statute of limitations is important, it very seldom arises in Small Claims Court. This is because most small claims cases are brought well within the accepted time limit. The following are the statutes of limitations in effect in Colorado for some types of actions:

One Year: Cases involving motor vehicle repair, and tort actions such as those based on assault or battery.

Two Years: Bad check cases in which triple damages are sought, and any type of action against health care providers, hospitals, pharmacies, dentists, optometrists, and veterinarians.

Three Years: Actions involving bodily injury or property damage arising out of a motor vehicle accident, contract cases, and those alleging fraud or misrepresentation.

Six Years: Actions to recover bad debts, unpaid loans, or for bad checks where triple damages are not sought.

CAN YOU SETTLE THIS?

Now that you are familiar with Small Claims Court, you should stop to consider the possibility of settling the case. Try to contact the other party directly. Describe for that person in a calm but firm tone how you have been damaged, and why you think the other party is liable for the damage. Perhaps the other person is quite aware that he or she is responsible, and has been waiting for you to call. You have nothing to lose by making this effort.

However, if nothing comes of this initial attempt to settle the issue, don't worry. You'll have more opportunities later on to talk settlement with the other party. Your job now is to let that person know that you take this matter seriously.

After you have determined that your case is appropriate for Small Claims Court—there is damage or loss, someone is liable, and the amount of the claim does not exceed $7,500— you are ready to proceed to court. The next chapter outlines how to initiate your small claims court case.

Chapter 3: Laying the Groundwork for a Small Claims Case

THE DEMAND LETTER

Now that you have determined that your case is appropriate for Small Claims Court, your first task is to lay the ground work for a successful outcome in court. One of the most effective ways to begin is to send the other party a letter outlining your version of the events in the case and asking for payment. This correspondence, sent by you directly to the other party without any court involvement, is usually called a demand letter.

The demand letter serves three important purposes. First, it helps you focus on the relevant aspects of the case before you initiate a court action. Composing a demand letter compels you to examine the facts in the case and determine the extent of the damage or loss, who is liable, and whether you want to pursue the case. A demand letter provides a good vehicle for clarifying what you intend to accomplish by filing an action.

Second, the demand letter serves to alert the other party to the fact that you believe he or she owes you money, without escalating the matter to the level of litigation. The other party is made aware of your seriousness as well. Sometimes, though not often, sending a demand letter will actually result in your receiving payment for your claim without the need for a formal court action. Count yourself among the very fortunate if your demand letter produces a settlement.

The third, and usually best, reason to send a demand letter prior to the commencement of a court action is to create a history of the case—from your perspective. The letter should state how you perceive the chronology of events thus far, and how you perceive the event, bargain, or transaction that is the basis for your claim. To this extent, the real audience for your demand letter is the judge, not the other party. You want to create a document that clearly sets out what has happened for the benefit of someone who has never heard of you or the other party and is totally unfamiliar with your dispute. This type of letter is especially important in a situation involving an oral contract, because it may be the only written account of the transaction.

Address the letter to the other party. The format of the typical demand letter begins with your account of the sequence of events. Start at the beginning, with the creation of the agreement or the details of the incident in question. Include all relevant information, but try not to stray from the central dispute. Do not include anything which does not advance your claim that the other party owes you.

Once you've established what happened and why the recipient of the letter should compensate you, tell that person what he or she needs to do to satisfy you. A clear request for compensation or action makes resolution of the case much easier for you, the other party and the judge.

After you've told the other party what must be done to satisfy you, establish a deadline for payment or action. The deadline should be reasonable, but not too long. Then tell the other party what additional damages, if any, you could incur if payment is not received by you before the deadline. This puts the other party on notice and acts as an additional incentive for the other party to settle.

As you write the letter, be mindful of the tone it conveys. There should be absolutely no threats of any kind in the letter, including that you will take the other party to court. The letter should be businesslike and level-headed. Let the judge see that you have been reasonable about the matter all along.

Send your demand letter to the other party via regular

mail. Be sure to make two copies for yourself, and note the date you mailed the letter. You now have evidence which will help your case later on.

Usually you will receive no reply at all to your letter. Don't worry—that really wasn't the point. Should you receive a phone call in response, be sure to write and send a confirmation letter to the other party as soon as possible. This letter should describe the contents of the phone conversation, the date, and who you spoke with. Again, by doing this, you are creating a record of the events of the case for the court to follow.

SAM'S CASE

After his phone conversation with Bob, Sam drafted and sent the following demand letter:

```
                    Sam Grant
                    Sam's Landscape Designs
                    15160 West McPherson Street
                    Golden, Colorado 80902
                    July 1, 2002

Mr. Robert Lee
1591 South Dahlia Street
Denver, Colorado 80224

Dear Mr. Lee,

     I am writing to request that you tender to
me the remaining balance due for the trees I
planted at your home on South Dahlia Street in
May of this year. The unpaid amount is $1,000.
     You will recall that I contacted you after
hearing from your work colleague, Mr. William T.
Sherman, of your interest in having some trees
planted in your yard. I phoned you to set up an
appointment on May 15, 2002, and we met at your
home on May 18. I offered to deliver and plant
four 5' Colorado Blue Spruce trees in your back-
yard for $2,000. You accepted this offer and
wrote me a check for $1,000 as a fifty percent
deposit for this service.
```

I planted the trees at your home on May 24.

I left with you an invoice for the remainder of the price, $1,000, and indicated that payment was due to me within two weeks.

Because I did not hear from you for over three weeks, I phoned you on June 16 requesting payment. You stated that recent financial problems had left you unable to pay anything at that time, and that you did not know when you would be able to pay the $1,000 you owe me.

I must now request that you send me the balance in full, $1,000, by July 20, 2002. You may forward this payment to me at the above address.

Yours truly,

Sam Grant

Sam Grant

If the deadline you set comes and goes without any response, much less payment, from the other party, you are now faced with a decision—should you proceed to file an action in Small Claims Court? While a case in Small Claims Court involves much less expense than litigation in other courts, you will still be called upon to make an investment of time and energy. Weigh this investment against the likelihood of your receiving payment. Consider what type of person the other party is. There are certain people who have no job and no assets, or who move around frequently, or who are just so slippery that collecting from them may be difficult at best.

But do not be discouraged just because your chances of obtaining full payment are not 100 percent. Remember the concept of perseverance, and that you are certain not to collect if you don't proceed.

Let's now examine how you go about filing an action in Small Claims Court.

Chapter 4: Filing an Action in Small Claims Court

WHERE TO SUE – VENUE

After you have determined that you are ready to proceed to Small Claims Court, your next step is to make the initial filing of court papers to begin the formal case. However, before you file any papers, you need to make sure you sue the other party in the correct Colorado county. Your case cannot go forward if it is not filed in the right court in the right place. This location issue goes by the legal term "venue."

The rules regarding actions in Small Claims Court are very specific about the proper place to bring the action. The case must be filed in a Colorado county in which at least one of the following requirements is met:

- the county where the other party resides

    or

- the county where the other party is regularly employed

    or

- the county where the other party is a student at an institution of higher education

    or

- the county where the other party has an office for the transaction of business

    or

25

- in landlord-tenant cases, the county in which the property is located.

The practical effect of these provisions concerning venue is that the damaged party must seek out the party liable for the damage, not the other way around. For example, if a resident of Arapahoe County damages your car when it is parked in front of your Adams County home, the small claims action will be initiated in Arapahoe County, unless you can show that the other party works, has an office, or attends college in Adams County. The county where the incident which resulted in the damage took place is not necessarily the proper location for a small claims filing. Rather, you must seek out the other party wherever he or she may be, regardless of the inconvenience to you. This inconvenience can be considerable, if, for example, you live in Durango and suffer damage caused by a resident of Denver.

Let's look more closely at each of the four venue options the Small Claims Court rules provide us. The first is the county in which the other party resides. For individual parties, this is relatively straightforward. The term "resides" is given its common-sense meaning, which is the place where the person primarily lives. The other party need not own property in that county, nor, conversely, does mere ownership of property in a county give rise to proper venue. A condominium in a mountain community, used by the other party only a handful of days a year, would not be considered that person's residence. However, a one-bedroom apartment in Castle Rock rented and lived in by the other party would suffice to make Douglas County an appropriate location in which to bring a small claims case.

It is not always an easy matter to determine in which county the other party resides even if you know his or her address. The city of Aurora, for instance, occupies portions of Adams, Arapahoe, and Douglas Counties, while Westminster sits in both Adams and Jefferson Counties. Make sure you know in which county a given address is located. A call to the county clerk should provide you with verification. Also remember that the location of a post office box mailing address is not necessarily in the same county as the person's actual residence.

The second possible venue in a small claims case is the county in which the other party is regularly employed. Again, this refers to individuals, and not to businesses or other entities.

If an individual works at a job five days a week, every week, in a given county, venue is proper and the case may be filed against that person in that county. If the other party is employed only part-time at a job in that county, but the employment is regular, you may sue there, too. There is no special minimum amount of time that establishes employment as "regular," but the longer the other party has been employed at the job in question, the better.

Venue is not proper under this provision in a situation in which the other party took on a special project in a county, completed it, and then went on to similar work in a neighboring county. A plumber working for a business in Denver sent to fix a leaky pipe in a house in Jefferson County would not be considered to be regularly employed in Jefferson County. This would be true even if this same plumber was assigned only to projects in Jefferson County. His county of regular employment would still be Denver County.

There are some people who live in Colorado but cannot be considered to be regularly employed in any Colorado county. Among these are persons who are truly unemployed, those whose employment is not regular, and individuals who work at home for a large company located in another state. These individuals will probably have to be sued in their county of residence.

The next possible location for bringing a small claims action is the county in which the other party is a student at an institution of higher learning. The thrust of this provision is to make it easier for those who have been somehow damaged by college students to sue such students in the county in which the college is located, rather than force them to travel to a distant county which the student claims as his or her residence. This means that a landlord in Greeley with tenants who damaged his apartment while attending the University of Northern Colorado could bring a small claims action in Weld County instead of the students' home county of Montrose, some three hundred miles away.

Remember that the county in question here is the county where the institution of higher learning is located, not the county where the student lives while attending the school. So, a student at Red Rocks Community College in Jefferson County who lives in Englewood but claims Delta County as her county of residence could be sued in the Small Claims Court in Jefferson County or Delta County, but not Arapahoe County.

Finally, you are safe giving the phrase "institution of higher learning" a broad meaning. Besides including universities and colleges, this term can also mean vocational schools, trade schools, or art schools.

Another venue option is the county where the other party has an office for the transaction of business. This will be the location where you could bring suit against a business, partnership, association, or corporation situated in that county. You may also sue an individual in that county if that person has an office where business is conducted. Again, view the phrase "has an office for the transaction of business" broadly enough to include a retail store, a restaurant, a doctor's office, a law office, a day care center, or any other site that could reasonably be considered a place of business. This office need not be continually bustling, or even open to the general public, for that matter. This provision is meant to be construed liberally so as to make the filing of a small claims case in the most logical location for all concerned as easy as possible. However, do notice that the language does not say that a county is the proper location if the other party merely "conducts" business there. The requirement is that there be an office in that county as well.

This option can serve to give those wondering where to bring a small claims action some choice. If you are suing a large business entity, they may have offices in many Colorado counties, any of which could be proper venue for a small claims suit. A fast-food chain which does not rely on franchisees may have a location in most counties in the state, making an action valid for filing in any of them.

Venue in a case involving a smaller business is often like that available when filing based on an individual's county of residence. Actions against these businesses must be brought in only one county, again regardless of the inconvenience to you. If you are a Denver resident hurt by the collapse of a table in a small restaurant in Alamosa, you will probably have to sue the restaurant in Alamosa County. We see again that the damaged party has the burden of seeking out the party responsible for damages.

In cases involving disputes between landlords and tenants, the case may be filed in the county in which the property that is the subject of the action is located. These cases typically involve either landlords suing tenants for damage done to a rental unit or tenants suing landlords for the return of a security deposit. Such cases may be brought in the county where the property is located even if that county cannot be the basis for the case based on any other criterion. However, this basis can only be used in a landlord-tenant dispute.

If you find yourself in a situation where two counties are permissible locations for a small claims action because the other party is a resident of County A and is regularly employed in County B, you may choose either one as the location for your suit. The other party will be forced to answer in the county you have chosen and may not have the case moved. Consider the case in which the party you wish to sue lives in Lakewood, is regularly employed part-time at a convenience store in Thornton, attends Metropolitan State College, and operates a bicycle repair shop on the weekends in Longmont. This person could be sued in Jefferson, Adams, Denver, or Boulder Counties, at your option.

The issue of timing needs to be raised here. The venue options are those in place at the time of the filing of the court action. For purposes of filing a case in Small Claims Court, the other party's county of residence, for example, is that county in which the other party lives on the day you file your case with the court. It is not necessarily the county where the other party lived at the time of the accident, when an apartment lease was signed, or when a bad check was written. If the other party lived in Denver when the damage incident occurred, but has since moved to Colorado Springs and continues to live there at the time you intend to file a court action, the other party's county of residence is considered to be El Paso County, not Denver County. The same timing rules apply to where the other party is employed, goes to college, or has an office.

On the downside, note that there are some people who you cannot bring in under any of the five venue categories. For example, someone who lives out-of-state and has no connection with Colorado cannot be sued in a Colorado Small Claims Court, even if they caused damage to you on the steps of the State Capitol Building. This is true even if a Colorado County Court or District Court is otherwise able to exert jurisdiction over the person. Small Claims Court rules specifically limit the possibilities. If none of the venue requirements can be met, then there can be no Small Claims Court action in this state, even if all the other requirements for a small claims action are in place.

There is one way in which you can potentially get around these venue requirements. The rules state that if a defendant appears and defends a small claims action on the merits at trial, the defendant shall be deemed to have waived any objection to the place of trial. So if you sue someone in the "wrong" county, but he or she shows up to defend the case anyway, the case may continue. Don't count on this happening, however.

LOCATION OF SMALL CLAIMS COURTS

After you have decided which county is best for your small claims action, you must go to the courthouse to file papers to initiate the case. Many courts do not allow you to file a small claims case over the phone or via a facsimile machine.

In most counties in Colorado, one courthouse serves as the location for both the District and County Courts, including Small Claims Court. A few counties are a bit trickier, however. The following is a list of the locations of Small Claims Courts in the larger counties in the state, at the time of this publication:

Adams County – The Adams County Justice Center is located at 1100 Judicial Center Drive in Brighton. Call (303) 654-3313 for more information.

Alamosa County – The courthouse is located at 4th and San Juan in Alamosa. The phone number is (719) 589-4996.

Arapahoe County – There are two locations where a small claims case may be filed in Arapahoe County. The County Court in Aurora is found at 15400 East 14th Place. Go to room 201 on the second floor. The phone number is (303) 363-8004.

The other County Court in Arapahoe County is in Littleton at 1790 West Littleton Boulevard. The phone number for information is (303) 798-4591.

Do not go to the newer courthouse on South Potomac Street in Englewood near Centennial Airport. Only the District Court is located there, and no small claims cases may be filed at this location.

If the person you want to sue can be sued in Arapahoe County under the venue rules discussed earlier, you are free to file either in Aurora or Littleton, no matter where in Arapahoe County the other party lives, works, or has an office.

Boulder County – Boulder County also has two locations at which a small claims case may be filed. The primary one is at the Boulder County Justice Center at 1777 Sixth Street at the corner of Sixth and Canyon. The phone number for County Court is (303) 441-4751.

There is also a County Court in Longmont which handles small claims cases. It is found at 1035 Kimbark Street, and can be reached by phone at (303) 682-6892. As with the two courts in Arapahoe County, you may file against someone who can be properly sued in Boulder County at either of these locations.

Broomfield County – Courts for the new City and County of Broomfield are located at 17 DesCombes Drive. The telephone number is (720) 887-2100.

Denver County – The Small Claims Court is not located in the City and County Building. Rather, it is found in a nondescript building about two blocks north at 1515 Cleveland Place. This building is directly behind, or to the east of, the Adam's Mark Hotel downtown, about 1/2 block south of the 16th Street Mall. The Clerk's Office is on the fourth floor. Call (303) 640-5161 for more information.

Douglas County – The courthouse is located at 4000 Justice Way, north of Castle Rock. The phone number is (303) 633-7200.

Eagle County – The Eagle County Justice Center is located at 885 Chambers Avenue in Eagle. Call (970) 328-6373 for more information.

El Paso County – The courthouse is located at 20 East Vermijo in downtown Colorado Springs. Small claims cases are filed in room 101 on the first floor. Call (719) 448-7636 for more information.

Garfield County – The courthouse is in Glenwood Springs at 109 8th Street. Small claims cases can be filed in Suite 104. The phone number is (970) 945-5075.

Jefferson County – Small Claims Court is held on the first floor of the Jefferson County Administrative and Courts Facility—known to some as the Taj Mahal—at 100 Jefferson County Parkway in Golden. When you enter the main lobby, turn right to the wing of the building that houses the courts. You can call (303) 271-6226 for more information.

LaPlata County – Small claims cases can be filed in Room 106 on the first floor of the courthouse at 1060 Second Avenue in Durango. The phone number is (970) 247-2004.

Larimer County – The Larimer County Justice Center is located in Fort Collins at 201 LaPorte Avenue. The phone number is (970) 498-7555.

Mesa County – Small claims cases are filed at the new courthouse located at 125 North Spruce in Grand Junction. Go to the annex behind the main building to find the County Court. More information is available at (970) 257-3640.

Montrose County – The courthouse address is 1200 Grand Avenue, Montrose. Small claims cases are filed in Room 210 on the second floor. The phone number for more information is (970) 252-4300.

Morgan County – The Morgan County Justice Center is located at 400 Warner in Fort Morgan. For more information, call (970) 8542-3414.

Otero County – File your small claims case in Room 105 of the Otero County Courthouse at 13 West Third Street in La Junta. Call (719) 384-4981 for more information.

Pueblo County – File your small claims case in room 101 on the first floor of the Judicial Center at Tenth and Grand in Pueblo. Do not go to the old Pueblo Courthouse building, which no longer houses the courts. Call (719) 583-7059 for more information.

Prowers County – Small claims cases are filed in the County Court clerk's office on the first floor of the courthouse, which is located at 301 South Main in Lamar. The phone number is (719) 336-7416.

Weld County – The courthouse is located in Greeley at the intersection of Ninth Avenue and Ninth Street. Enter through the south door, and proceed to the north end of the first floor for the small claims window. The phone number is (970) 351-7300, extension 4531.

FILING A SMALL CLAIMS CASE

Now that you know where to file your case, it's time to get the necessary paperwork, complete it, and get the legal process started. Go to the Clerk's Office in the County Court of the county where you have decided to file suit. If there is a window or counter in the Clerk's Office which says "Small Claims," go there first. Otherwise, just go to the main counter in the County Court Clerk's Office. Keep in mind that you want the clerk of the County Court, not the County Clerk, who takes care of things like license plates for that county.

Tell the clerk that you are interested in filing a small claims case and that you would like a copy of the form necessary to begin a case. The clerk should provide you with the form, and may also give you an informational packet about filing small claims cases in that court. Some courts provide these packets free of charge, while others assess a nominal fee.

You may see a sign in the clerk's office which reads "court

personnel are not allowed to give legal advice. Please do not ask." This less-than-friendly sign is notice to you that court clerks cannot give you any help with the legal aspects of your case. To do so would be practicing law without a license.

It is not always easy to determine exactly where simple assistance ends and legal advice begins. The kinds of questions court personnel cannot help you with are those which deal with the facts in your particular case, such as issues of liability, the amount of damage, and whether someone is a resident of the county. You must answer these questions on your own.

However, the court personnel should answer general questions such as those relating to the filing of forms, service, when hearings are held, and other procedural matters. If you have trouble getting answers to questions like these, keep asking. Remember that perseverance is important in small claims cases, and it may be called for in this situation.

Small Claims Court, _____ **1** _____ County, Colorado
Court Address:

PLAINTIFF(S): _____ **2** _____
Address: _____ **3** _____
City/State/Zip: _____
Phone: Home _____ Work _____
v.
DEFENDANT (1): _____ **4** _____
Address: _____ **5** _____
City/State/Zip: _____
Phone: Home _____ **6** _____ Work _____
DEFENDANT (2): _____ **7** _____
Address: _____
City/State/Zip: _____
Phone: Home _____ Work _____

▲ **COURT USE ONLY** ▲

Case Number:

Division: Courtroom:

NOTICE, CLAIM AND SUMMONS TO APPEAR FOR TRIAL (Part 1)

If Defendant(s) is/are other than a person, call the Secretary of State's office at (303) 894-2251, or go on-line at www.sos.state.co.us to determine the registered agent for service of this notice. Please enter name and address of the agent.
Name: _____ **8** _____
Address: _____
The Defendant(s) is/are in the military service: ☐ Yes ☐ No **9** I am an attorney: ☐ Yes ☐ No **10**
The Defendant(s) reside(s), is/are regularly employed, has/have an office for the transaction of business, or is/are a student in this county, or the Defendant(s) own(s) the rental property in the county that is the subject of this claim. ☐ Yes ☐ No **11**
I/We understand that it is my/our responsibility to provide the court with proof that the Defendant(s) has/have been served 15 days prior to the trial. ☐ Yes ☐ No **12**

NOTICE AND SUMMONS TO APPEAR FOR TRIAL

To the Defendant(s): **13**
You are scheduled to have your trial in this case on (date) _____ (time) _____ at the Court address stated in the above caption. Bring with you all books, papers and witnesses you need to establish your defense. **IF YOU DO NOT APPEAR, JUDGMENT WILL BE ENTERED AGAINST YOU.** If you wish to defend the claim or present a counterclaim, you must provide a written response or written counterclaim on the scheduled trial date and pay a **NONREFUNDABLE** filing fee.

Dated: _____
_____
Clerk of Court/Deputy

PLAINTIFF(S)'S CLAIM
The Defendant(s) owe(s) me $_____ **14** _____, which includes penalties, plus interest and costs allowed by law, and/or should be ordered to return property, perform a contract or set aside a contract or comply with a restrictive covenant for the following reasons. (Please describe the property being requested).
15
_____
_____
_____
_____
_____
_____

Note: The combined value of money, property, specific performance or cost to remedy a covenant violation cannot exceed $7,500.00.

I/We declare under penalty of perjury that the above statements are true and correct, and that I/we have not filed more than two claims in any one or more small claims courts in Colorado during this month, nor more than 18 claims in this calendar year.

Dated: _____
_____ **16** _____
Plaintiff's Signature

_____
Plaintiff's Signature

JDF 250 R9/01 (Part 1) NOTICE, CLAIM AND SUMMONS TO APPEAR FOR TRIAL

COMPLETING THE COMPLAINT

The form you will receive from the clerk is No. JDF 250, *Notice, Claim, and Summons to Appear for Trial*, also known as the "complaint." It is a four-part form with three different colored copies under the top page. At the top, it advises you to press hard when filing out the form. This is good advice. You may complete the form with a pen or a typewriter, though the latter is preferable because it makes the copies easier to read. If you complete the form with a pen, remember to write very clearly and legibly.

Let's look now at the various pieces of information you will need to complete this form:

1. Fill in the county name and address of the court if the form does not already contain this information.

2. Your name, or the name of your business or other entity, if it is the one that has suffered the damage. If there are multiple parties suing, list each by name.

3. If you are suing as an individual, use your residential address. If your business or other group is suing, use its office address and phone number. Do not use a post office box number.

4. If you are suing an individual, use the individual's full name here. Include any aliases you are aware of. If you are suing two or more individuals, list each. If you are suing a business, put its name here. If you are not sure if you should file against the individual or the business, list both. For example, it is perfectly acceptable to list "Michael A. Jones" and "Mike's Auto Repair Shop." You may also use the abbreviation "d/b/a," which stands for "doing business as," in this situation, as in "Michael A. Jones, d/b/a Mike's Auto Repair Shop." If you are suing a partnership, list the business name and all partners. If you are not sure who the owner of a business is, call the city or county tax office or the state Department of Revenue. They can find the owner of a business based on tax records. This information can be critical, and can help you determine if a business is owned by a separate corporation, such as the X Corporation doing business as the "Corner Bar. "

5. Even though you can list more than one item on the name line, you must have only one address here. Use the address which corresponds to the venue option which led you to file the action in that county. If you are suing in Jefferson County because it is the other person's county of residence, list that person's residential address. However, if you choose the county where the person is employed or has an office, list the address where he or she works or maintains an office. A post office box is not acceptable. Call the post office to ascertain the mailing address of the person using this post office box.

6. List the appropriate phone number or numbers if you know them.

7. Space is provided for you to include information regarding a second defendant, if there is one in your case.

8. If you are suing an individual, you may leave this portion of the form blank. If you are suing a corporation, call the Colorado Secretary of State's Office at (303) 894-2251 to get the name and address of the corporation's registered agent. This is the person who will receive your legal papers on behalf of the corporation. If you are unsure if a business is a corporation, try the Secretary of State anyway to see if the business has a registered agent listed. If the business is a sole proprietorship or a partnership, it will not have a named registered agent, and you need not complete this section of the form. Information regarding registered agents is also available at the Secretary of State's website at www.sos.state.co.us.

9. This box is on the form because federal and state law protect active duty members of the military against default judgments. The court needs to know if the other party is in fact a serviceman or woman. Do not check the "yes" box if the other party is in the reserves. If you sue someone who is in the military and he or she is served and shows up for the hearing, the case will proceed normally. However, no judgment will be granted if the other party is on active military duty but does not appear for the hearing. If you know that the

defendant is in the military, check "yes". If the person is only in the reserves, check "no", as this is inactive duty.

10. Attorneys may bring actions on their own behalf in Small Claims Court, but they must make the other party aware of the fact that they have legal training. Even an attorney who no longer practices law must mark the "yes" box.

11. You cannot file a small claims case if you cannot answer yes to this question. The court wants to make sure you know the rules before it considers your case.

12. The court is reminding you of the requirements you will have to meet regarding serving the other party with a copy of the complaint. You must mark the "Yes" box.

13. The court clerk will complete this section when your case is set for hearing.

14. Fill in the amount you wish to claim from the other party here. While you should ask for all actual damages amounting to less than $7,500, do not include costs related to preparing the case, such as expenses for phone calls or for making copies of documents. Be sure to include everything else, though, because you probably won't be awarded a judgment for any amount you have not asked for. If you are seeking triple damages for a bad check, and have met the notice requirements described in Chapter 3, your claim is for the tripled amount, or at least $100, not the face value of the check.

15. Here is where you state your case in a nutshell. The court wants to know the basic nature of your claim. While it is important to be complete, do not feel you need to ramble, put in every detail, or fill in all three lines to win your case. Statements like "Ms. Wilson failed to return my security deposit for an apartment I rented from her from July 2001 to July 2002" or "The Westside Appliance Repair Shop did not adequately complete repairs on my refrigerator as agreed" are quite acceptable. The point is to let everyone, especially the court and the other party, know why you are suing. You will have the opportunity to go into more detail later in the actual hearing.

16. Do not forget to sign and date this form. Notarization is not required. All parties listed in item two must sign. If you are a corporation, your corporate officer should sign.

FILING FEES

After you have completed the complaint form, go back to the appropriate small claims counter and tell the clerk you would like to file your case. It is at this time that you will face the first of a possible series of fees which often come with the successful pursuit of a case in Small Claims Court. The first is the filing fee, and it is paid by the person filing the case based on the amount you are asking for in your complaint, as follows:

Amount of Claim	Filing Fee
$500 and below	$ 9.00
$500.01 to $7500	$23.00

These fees are non-refundable. You will not get your money back if you change your mind or if you settle with the other party without ever going to trial.

After you pay this fee, the clerk will return all but one of the copies of the complaint to you. Do not lose these other copies. You will need the other copies for service on the other party.

THE HEARING DATE

The next item of business is setting the date for the court hearing. The clerk will offer you the next possible date, but you can request a later one if that one is more convenient for you. Be sure the date is at least 30 days from the date you file. This amount of time is needed to provide sufficient time for the service of your complaint and response by the other party. In most courts, however, this will not be an issue. Expect your court date to be set between six and ten weeks from the date you file.

You should also be aware of the different days of the week and times of day different courts hold small claims hearings. The following is a list of the usual schedule of small claims hearings (at the time of this publication) in the largest courts in Colorado, as well as the length of time you can expect to wait for a hearing:

Adams County – Hearings may be held on any day of the week. The wait for a hearing date is about three months.

Alamosa County – Small claims cases are heard on Mondays, beginning at 10 a.m. Cases are usually set for hearing approximately 30 to 40 days after they are filed.

Arapahoe County – Small claims cases are heard on Wednesday and Thursday evenings starting at 6:30 p.m., and on Saturdays in Littleton. Cases are heard about two months after they are filed.

Cases filed in Aurora are set for hearing in two months or so, and are heard on Mondays and Tuesdays.

Broomfield County – Cases are heard on Fridays about one month after filing.

Boulder County – Cases are heard in Boulder on Mondays, Tuesdays, Thursdays, and Fridays from 9 a.m. until 2:30 p.m. Hearings are set for about six weeks from the date of filing.

In Longmont, cases are set for hearing about six weeks after they are filed, with the hearings taking place on Thursdays between 9:30 a.m. and 2:30 p.m.

Denver County – Small claims cases are heard Monday through Friday beginning at 8 a.m. and continuing until 3 p.m. Hearings are usually scheduled for about six weeks from the filing date.

Douglas County – Cases are scheduled for Mondays, and are set for at least eight months after the filing date.

Eagle County – Small Claims Court holds hearings on Monday mornings and Wednesday afternoons. Hearings are scheduled about two months after cases are filed.

El Paso County – Cases are heard at various times during the week and on Saturdays. Expect a hearing date set about six to eight weeks after filing.

Garfield County – Hearings for small claims cases

are heard on Thursdays, and are typically held about six weeks after filing.

Jefferson County – Cases are heard between 6:30 p.m. and 9:30 p.m. Monday through Thursday. Hearings are scheduled for about six weeks from the date of filing.

LaPlata County – Cases in Small Claims Court begin at 8:30 a.m. on Thursdays. Expect your hearing to be set for about six weeks after you file.

Larimer County – Small claims hearings are held on Fridays, starting at 8:30 a.m. The wait for a hearing is about two months.

Mesa County – Small claims cases are heard at various times depending on the demand. They are set for hearing about three months after filing.

Montrose County – Small claims cases are generally heard on the first Monday of each month, starting at 1:30 p.m. They are usually set for hearing about six weeks after cases are filed.

Morgan County – Small claims cases are heard on Monday, Wednesday, and Thursday mornings. Cases are usually set for hearing about one month after they are filed.

Otero County – Cases are heard on Mondays and Wednesdays. Your case will be set for about six weeks after filing.

Prowers County – Hearings are held on Fridays starting at 9:00 a.m. Hearing dates are set for about one month after cases are filed.

Pueblo County – Cases are scheduled for Monday, Wednesday, and Friday at 9:00 a.m. The hearing will be held about two months after the filing date.

Weld County – Cases are usually heard on Monday, Tuesday, Wednesday, and Friday. Your case can be heard about six weeks after filing.

These dates and times are subject to change, so please check with the court when filing. Other courts in Colorado generally schedule small claims cases less frequently. The County Court in other locations can provide you with this information.

LIMITATIONS ON CASE FILINGS

The law regarding Small Claims Court does contain a limit on the number of cases a person can file in a given time period. This limitation is meant to discourage the filing of frivolous and harassing actions.

No plaintiff may file more than two claims per month, or more than eighteen claims per calendar year, in the Small Claims Court of any county. The complaint form includes language to this effect, and requires that the plaintiff attest that he has not violated these provisions.

This limitation is slightly different for one class of plaintiffs. A state-supported institution of higher education filing to recover amounts due on loans or other outstanding obligations owed to it may file up to thirty small claims cases per month in all Small Claims Courts in the state.

SERVICE OF PROCESS

After your case has been filed, your next task is to let the other party know that you are suing him or her. Now that you have filed a formal legal action, you are now considered the "plaintiff" and the party you are suing is the "defendant." The legal system requires that the defendant be made aware of the legal action brought against him or her. This is accomplished via the "service" of legal "process" on the defendant. In plain English, this means that the legal papers initiating the suit must be delivered to the defendant. While the legal rules in some areas are more relaxed in Small Claims Court than they are in a traditional court setting, you are still constrained by the formal rules when it comes to service of process. Remember, proper service acts as proof to the court that the defendant had formal notice of your claim. Without proof of service, your case may not proceed.

The legal rules regarding service of process are quite specific. Keep in mind that service means actual service of the legal papers on the defendant, not just awareness of your legal action by the other party. It is not good enough that you heard that the defendant knows you have filed suit. It is not good enough that you called the defendant and told him of the case. It is not even good enough if you told the other party face-to-face, in person, that you have filed suit for $700 and that the court hearing is set for the 25th of next month at 10:00 a.m. It is your responsibility to ensure that the defendant—or each defendant if you are suing more than one person—is properly served according to the rules.

The first thing you must be aware of is that you, the plaintiff, may not serve the complaint yourself. You are an interested party in the case, with a financial stake in its outcome, and the law views this fact as providing sufficient incentive to someone in your position to be untruthful about whether the defendant was ever served. Fairness—and the law—dictates that a more neutral party must serve the defendant.

The law provides four ways for you to serve notice on the defendant. The first is to have the court send the yellow copy of the complaint to the defendant via certified mail. The advantage of this option is that it is relatively cheap—about $5—and you need not do any of the work. The downside is that the defendant can sometimes easily avoid being served merely by failing to pick up the certified letter at the post office. This is especially true if you are suing someone who has been through the system before. These "professional defendants" know that a certified letter probably means trouble for them. Worse yet, it may be two or three weeks later before the post office lets you and the court know that the intended recipient has not picked up the letter. Without a return receipt card signed by the defendant from the post office showing that the defendant received the paperwork, the case cannot continue. However, if the defendant refuses to accept the certified letter—as opposed to just ignoring the notice to pick it up—the post office will note this formal refusal on the return receipt card. In this situation, the other party's refusal of service by certified mail is as good as real service.

If you have no reason to suspect that the defendant will attempt to dodge a certified letter, this method may be worth a try. You should tell the court clerk you want to serve the defendant via certified mail at the same time you file your case. You must pay the clerk the service fee at this time.

One final word of caution needs to be raised regarding service by certified mail. Even though the rules expressly allow for service in this manner, many judges and magistrates in Small Claims Court frown upon its use. They view it as inherently unreliable, and are not comfortable granting judgments in cases where the defendant does not appear at the hearing if service was done this way. Feel free to ask the clerk when you file your case how the judge or magistrate in that court feels about this issue. The clerk may even tell you what form of service the court recommends in small claims cases.

The second method for serving process involves the county sheriff. A deputy will attempt to serve your papers for a fee of around $20. Some sheriffs will make you pay in advance, while others will send you a bill after they have attempted to serve the defendant. You must take your papers directly to the sheriff's office in the county in which you want the defendant served. The deputy will attempt to serve the defendant at the address you provide sometime between the hours of 8 a.m. and 5 p.m. If successful, the sheriff will complete the bottom portion of the green copy of the complaint and return it to you. Proof of service provided by the sheriff's office is considered by most judges to be the most reliable.

The advantage of service by the sheriff, besides the reliability, is that many who would think nothing of refusing to pick up a certified letter find it much more difficult to evade a sheriff trying to serve them. There are people who will still avoid service this way. Unfortunately, if the first attempt at service by a sheriff is not successful, you must pay again for additional attempts. The sheriff's office has no real financial incentive to complete the service because it gets paid whether service is successful or not.

The next option is to use a private process server. There are businesses whose primary source of income is fees paid by private parties for process serving. The Denver Yellow Pages lists almost 50 such operations. Just look under "Process Servers." You can expect to pay about $25 to $35, plus mileage. The advantage here is that these firms will cross county lines to find the defendant, and, because they usually do not get paid unless service is successful, they have an economic incentive to actually serve the defendant. This means they are not limited to an 8 to 5 schedule, and that they may be more creative in their service attempts than the sheriff. Be sure to inquire about the fees a process serving firm charges before you decide to use one.

The last option is to have someone you know serve the defendant. The law allows anyone at least eighteen years old who is not a party to the action nor a member of the plaintiff's family to serve the defendant. This person must actually serve the defendant in person by first announcing "this is a summons and complaint for a lawsuit" and then handing the defendant's copy of the complaint to the defendant. If the defendant jumps back or resists, the server must still "tag" the defendant with the papers.

While this option can be the least expensive method of personally serving the defendant, it is also considered the least reliable by the courts. If you decide to go this route, be sure your process server is aware of the rules regarding proper service. Remind this person to complete the Certificate of Personal Service portion of the green copy of the complaint, including the notarization section and return it to you. Remember, this is what the judge will examine later to determine if service was proper so that your case may proceed.

Your process server, be it the sheriff, a private firm, or your best friend, can get around the requirement for personal service on the defendant in two ways. First, the law allows service on the defendant via service of the complaint at the defendant's primary residence on any person over age eighteen who regularly resides there. If you know where the defendant maintains a primary residence, your chosen process server may go to that house and give the yellow copy of the complaint to the defendant's spouse or roommate. Delivery to an underage child or visitor to that home is not acceptable.

The second way around the personal service requirement is service at the defendant's place of business by leaving the complaint with the person's "secretary, bookkeeper, chief clerk, office receptionist or assistant, or business partner." What this language means is that you can have your process server go to the defendant's place of employment or office and effect service by leaving the defendant's copy of the complaint there with the proper person. It must be left with someone who is in a position of authority in that office or has some sort of special status with the defendant.

Special service rules apply to certain defendants. If you are suing a minor, you must serve the minor *and* the minor's mother, father, or legal guardian either personally or by certified mail. Personal service in this situation may be done by delivering a copy of the complaint to any person in whose care or control the minor may be, or with whom the minor resides, or in whose service the minor is employed. If you are suing a partnership, limited liability company, limited partnership, or other unincorporated association, you must serve a partner, limited partner, manager, officer, or general agent by delivering a copy of the papers to the entity's receptionist, office manager, or bookkeeper.

To sue a private corporation, you must serve the papers on an officer of the corporation, a manager, receptionist, legal assistant, paid legal adviser, or general agent. The general agent is the individual listed with the Secretary of State as the official registered agent in Colorado for that corporation. This is the person you listed in item number eight of the *Notice, Claim, and Summons to Appear for Trial*. What this may mean is that you may be serving the complaint on the corporation in a different county than you are using as the basis for your venue. It is perfectly acceptable for you to sue if a corporation has an office for the transaction of business in Greeley, but the registered agent's office is in Fort Collins. Simply file your case in Weld County and have the registered agent served in Larimer County.

If you are suing a state or local governmental entity, follow these rules for personal service. To sue a county, deliver the papers to the county clerk and recorder or chief deputy of the county attorney for that county. For a school district, serve the complaint on the superintendent, assistant superintendent, clerk, or a director of the school district. To sue the state, deliver the papers to the office of the Attorney General in Denver and to a designated employee of the agency in question.

If your action involves a dispute over a security deposit, you may deliver a copy of the papers to the owner of the property or to a person or firm authorized to accept security deposits or rent payments on behalf of the owner of the property.

Whatever method of service you choose, bear in mind that successful service must be **completed** at least fifteen calendar days prior to the date set for the trial. If service is not completed by that date, you must start all over again with a new hearing date. Make sure you get the green copy of the complaint back from your process server with the Certificate of Personal Service completed and notarized. Unless you were successful in serving the defendant via certified mail, you may have to produce this Certificate at the court hearing to prove to the judge that the defendant was properly served with your complaint. Make a copy of this form immediately, and do not lose it.

SAM'S CASE

After one month, Sam had received no reply from Bob to his July 1 demand letter. He decided to pursue his claim in Small Claims Court.

Sam first set about determining where he should sue Bob. He knew Bob's primary residence was in Denver County at the house where Sam had planted the trees. He also knew from his neighbor, Billy T., who was Bob's co-worker, that Bob was employed at the Thornton Glass Company in Adams County. He did not believe Bob maintained any sort of office anywhere, and was doubtful that Bob was enrolled as a college student.

Sam could sue Bob either in Denver County or Adams County. Because the Adams County courthouse in Brighton was more than thirty miles from his home in Golden, Sam decided to file his case in Denver.

Sam obtained the complaint form from the clerk's office in Denver County Court. He completed the form, paid his filing fee of $23, and was assigned a court date of October 2nd. Sam also decided to have the court serve Bob via certified mail, and he paid the accompanying fee of $4.80.

Small Claims Court, _____ County, Colorado
Court Address:

PLAINTIFF(S): Sam Grant, d/b/a Sam's Landscape Designs
Address: 151600 W. McPherson Avenue
City/State/Zip: Golden, CO 80419
Phone: Home 303-555-1111   Work 303-555-2222
v.
DEFENDANT (1): Robert Lee
Address: 1591 S. Dahlia Street
City/State/Zip: Denver, CO 80224
Phone: Home 303-555-3333   Work 303-555-4444
DEFENDANT (2): _____
Address: _____
City/State/Zip: _____
Phone: Home _____ Work _____

▲ COURT USE ONLY ▲
Case Number:
Division: Courtroom:

NOTICE, CLAIM AND SUMMONS TO APPEAR FOR TRIAL (Part 1)

If Defendant(s) is/are other than a person, call the Secretary of State's office at (303) 894-2251, or go on-line at www.sos.state.co.us to determine the registered agent for service of this notice. Please enter name and address of the agent.
Name: _____ N/A
Address: _____
The Defendant(s) is/are in the military service: ☐ Yes ☒ No   I am an attorney: ☐ Yes ☒ No
The Defendant(s) reside(s), is/are regularly employed, has/have an office for the transaction of business, or is/are a student in this county, or the Defendant(s) own(s) the rental property in the county that is the subject of this claim. ☒ Yes ☐ No
I/We understand that it is my/our responsibility to provide the court with proof that the Defendant(s) has/have been served 15 days prior to the trial. ☒ Yes ☐ No

NOTICE AND SUMMONS TO APPEAR FOR TRIAL
To the Defendant(s):
You are scheduled to have your trial in this case on (date) _____ (time) _____ at the Court address stated in the above caption. Bring with you all books, papers and witnesses you need to establish your defense. **IF YOU DO NOT APPEAR, JUDGMENT WILL BE ENTERED AGAINST YOU.** If you wish to defend the claim or present a counterclaim, you must provide a written response or written counterclaim on the scheduled trial date and pay a **NONREFUNDABLE** filing fee.

Dated: _____
    Clerk of Court/Deputy

PLAINTIFF(S)'S CLAIM
The Defendant(s) owe(s) me $ 1,000.00 , which includes penalties, plus interest and costs allowed by law, and/or should be ordered to return property, perform a contract or set aside a contract or comply with a restrictive covenant for the following reasons. (Please describe the property being requested):

I planted trees valued at $2,000.00 on Mr. Lee's property under the terms of a verbal agreement.
He paid $1,000.00 but now refuses to pay the remaining $1,000.00 owed.

Note: The combined value of money, property, specific performance or cost to remedy a covenant violation cannot exceed $7,500.00.

I/We declare under penalty of perjury that the above statements are true and correct, and that I/we have not filed more than two claims in any one or more small claims courts in Colorado during this month, nor more than 18 claims in this calendar year.

Dated: August 15, 2002   *Sam Grant*
    Plaintiff's Signature

    Plaintiff's Signature

JDF 250 R9/01 (Part 1) NOTICE, CLAIM AND SUMMONS TO APPEAR FOR TRIAL

Sam called the court two weeks later to see if the return of service receipt card with Bob's signature had been received by the court. Sam gave the court clerk his case number, but the clerk reported that no return card had been placed in the case file.

Three days later, Sam received a postcard from the court in the mail. It was entitled Notice of No Service and listed his name, Bob's name, and the small claims case number. It informed Sam that the attempted service by mail on Bob was not successful, and that Sam would have to make personal service on Bob under the rules of Small Claims Court. Sam would have to try again.

Small Claims Court, _____ Denver _____ County, Colorado Court Address: **PLAINTIFF(S):** _ Sam Grant, d/b/a Sam's Landscape Designs _ Address: __ 151600 W. McPherson Avenue __ City/State/Zip: _ Golden, CO 80419 _ Phone: Home __ 303-555-1111 ___ Work _ 303-555-2222 _ v. **DEFENDANT(S):** __ Robert Lee __ Address: __ 1591 S. Dahlia Street __ City/State/Zip: _ Denver, CO 80224 _ Phone: Home __ 303-555-3333 ___ Work _ 303-555-4444 _	 ▲ **COURT USE ONLY** ▲ Case Number: 02 S 991 Division: Courtroom:

NOTICE OF NO SERVICE

TO THE PLAINTIFF(S):

PLEASE BE ADVISED that the attempted service by mail of the Notice, Claim and Summons to Appear for Trial upon the Defendant(s) was unsuccessful. If you desire to pursue this case, you are required to obtain an "Alias Notice, Claim and Summons to Appear for Trial" from the Clerk of the Court. You must have the Defendant personally served at least 15 days prior to the first scheduled trial date as set forth in the Alias Notice, Claim and Summons to Appear for Trial.

Date: _____   _____
                                              Clerk of Court/Deputy Clerk

---

CERTIFICATE OF MAILING

I hereby certify that on (date) _____, I mailed a true and correct copy of the NOTICE OF NO SERVICE, by placing it in the United States Mail, postage pre-paid to the parties at the addresses listed above.

Date: _____   _____
                                              Clerk of Court/Deputy Clerk

Because it was now September, Sam realized he only had a short time in which to serve Bob with the papers for the legal action. If the papers were not successfully served by September 17, the requirement that Bob be served at least fifteen days prior to the court date would not be met. Failure to serve Bob by then would force Sam to get a later hearing date.

Sam decided to try a private process server. He called the number he found in the phone book for "Long Arm Process Servers, Inc." in Denver. They agreed to attempt service right away. Their fee was $30 plus 25 cents per mile. Sam delivered the yellow copy of the complaint to their office. He also provided them with Bob's work and home addresses, as well as his physical description.

Sam was relieved when a representative from Long Arm called to say that Bob had been served at his office on Monday, September 16. The company mailed Sam a bill for $34 and the completed and notarized Certificate of Personal Service on the green copy of the complaint.

Now Sam was officially a plaintiff and Bob a defendant.

JUDGE OR MAGISTRATE?

Courts in the larger counties in Colorado have for many years had to deal with caseloads which significantly exceed the number of judges available to hear cases and render decisions. To meet the demands associated with a constantly increasing number of cases filed each year, courts have relied on judicial officers called "magistrates" to preside over cases which do not always require the authority of an appointed judge. Magistrates are utilized by both County Courts and District Courts, and hear cases involving traffic offenses, child support, and juvenile delinquency, as well as other areas of the law. In many locations, magistrates also hear small claims cases.

Some courts will automatically assign your case to be heard by a magistrate. A magistrate in Small Claims Court has the same powers as a judge, and the magistrate's ruling is the decision of the court. As a practical matter, it will make little difference to you whether your case is heard by a judge or by a magistrate.

You are, however, allowed to have your case heard by a judge rather than a magistrate. You may make this request by obtaining form No. JDF 259 *Objection to Magistrate Hearing Case* from the clerk's office. Just complete the form and hand it to the clerk when you file your case, or at any time at least seven days before the court date. You need not state a reason for your objection. Requesting a judge may result in pushing back the date of your hearing until such time as a judge is available. Plaintiffs should also be aware that the defendant has a similar right to object to a magistrate hearing the case, and may make a similar request demanding the case be heard by a judge. This, too, could have the effect of moving back the hearing date. You will be informed if it is changed as a result of a request by the defendant.

One thing you do not have to worry about is whether to ask for a jury in your case. Jury trials are not allowed in Small Claims Court.

Now that your case has been filed, let's examine the possible actions the defendant may now take in response.

Small Claims Court, _____ County, Colorado Court Address:	
PLAINTIFF(S): _____ Address: _____ City/State/Zip: _____ Phone: Home _____ Work _____ v. **DEFENDANT(S):** _____ Address: _____ City/State/Zip: _____ Phone: Home _____ Work _____	▲ **COURT USE ONLY** ▲ Case Number: Division: Courtroom:

OBJECTION TO MAGISTRATE HEARING CASE

I, _____, am the ☐ PLAINTIFF ☐ DEFENDANT in this case, and I object to a magistrate hearing the above captioned case, and pursuant to C.R.C.P. 511, I request that this case be heard by a judge.

I understand that this motion must be filed at least seven days before the trial date stated on the Notice, Claim, Summons to Appear for Trial.

Date: _____

_____
Signature of ☐ PLAINTIFF ☐ DEFENDANT

NOTICE TO PARTIES:

You are notified that, at the request of the above-signed party, this case will be heard by a judge instead of a magistrate.

☐ There is no change in the trial date of _____.
☐ There is a new trial date of _____.
☐ See attached trial notice form.

Date: _____

_____
Clerk of Court/Deputy Clerk

CERTIFICATE OF MAILING

I hereby certify that on (date)_____, I mailed a true and correct copy of the OBJECTION TO MAGISTRATE HEARING CASE, by placing it in the United States Mail, postage pre-paid to the parties at the addresses listed above.

_____
Clerk of Court/Deputy Clerk

JDF 259 R9/01 OBJECTION TO MAGISTRATE HEARING CASE

Chapter 5: The Defendant's Response

WHAT THE DEFENDANT MUST KNOW

Much of the information for plaintiffs contained in this book also applies to defendants. Both should be aware of the venue rules, the various filing fees, as well as the methods for calculating damages. The later discussions concerning the use of witnesses, the role of evidence in the trial, and one's demeanor in court are equally applicable to each party. In short, defendants can also benefit by becoming acquainted with the workings of Small Claims Court.

THE DEFENDANT'S OPTIONS

When a defendant has been successfully served with a summons and complaint, he is officially on notice that a small claims action has commenced. The defendant also knows when and where the court hearing is scheduled to take place.

At this point, the defendant has to choose how to respond to the claims that have been made and may do any of the following.

- The defendant may decide to do nothing at all in response to the plaintiff's claims.
- The defendant can file a response indicating that he does not believe anything is owed by the defendant.
- The defendant can respond by upping the ante through the filing of a counterclaim against the plaintiff.

- The defendant may wish to be represented by an attorney and seek to move the case out of Small Claims Court.
- The defendant could contact the plaintiff in hopes of settling the case before the date of the hearing.
- The defendant could request mediation of the matter.

Let's look more closely at each of these possible responses by the defendant and what they mean for the plaintiff.

SETTLEMENT

Perhaps the best response the plaintiff can hope for is some communication from the defendant as a result of the plaintiff's formal legal complaint. Certainly the fact that a small claims case was filed conveys to the other party how serious the plaintiff considers the matter to be. A defendant might try to reach some kind of agreement prior to the scheduled court date.

Should the defendant choose this course of action, it is usually in the plaintiff's best interests to at least consider the idea of a settlement. After all, the goal of this whole process is to collect some measure of compensation for the damages, not to prevail over the defendant in the court case. The plaintiff should take seriously any offer of settlement made by the defendant, even if it is for an amount less than he is seeking in the formal complaint. In many instances, taking less now can save everyone headaches in the future.

If the parties agree to a settlement, be sure the agreement is in writing. This assures both parties that they each understand the other and what is being agreed to by each of them. The written agreement also provides a tangible piece of evidence if there is trouble down the road. The written settlement agreement need not be anything fancy or complicated. Simply spell out the terms of the agreement and get dated signatures from all parties. A form No. 348, *Release and Settlement of Claim,* found at Bradford Publishing Company in Denver, might be used for this purpose.

If the parties are able to achieve a settlement, the plaintiff can proceed in one of two ways. He can send a copy of the agreement to the court where he filed the case, with a cover letter indicating that the dispute was settled and therefore no longer needs a court hearing. The court will then dismiss the action.

The other option is for the plaintiff to show up at the scheduled court hearing with a copy of the settlement agreement in hand and explain the situation to the judge or magistrate. The judge should look favorably upon the request for a judgment and will more than likely enter judgment against the defendant as called for in the agreement.

MEDIATION

You may also consider mediation. This is a procedure that takes place outside the court process. It allows you to sit down with the other party in an effort to reach a mutually satisfactory agreement regarding the dispute. The mediator is not there to force a settlement, but, rather, to assist the parties in creating a settlement. In this way, both parties can feel that they have a stake in the final agreement, thus increasing the chances of its provisions being adhered to. Many defendants will respond more favorably to a mediated settlement than to a judgment forced on them by the Small Claims Court.

There are many organizations in Colorado which offer mediation services. The court system operates the Office of Dispute Resolution, which offers trained mediators to assist with almost any type of dispute at many locations around the state. You can also get a referral from the Colorado Council of Mediators and Mediation Organizations. Finally, you can try the yellow pages under "mediation".

REQUEST FOR A NEW HEARING DATE

The defendant may ask the court to change the hearing date if the original date is inconvenient for the defendant. This request must be made by the defendant at least seven days prior to the scheduled hearing date. If the new hearing date is granted, the court will notify the plaintiff of the new date and time.

DEFENSES

The defendant can challenge the small claims action without addressing any of the actual issues raised in the claim. This is done by questioning the procedures by which the suit was begun.

The defendant can argue that he was never served with the complaint, or that he was served improperly, or that the papers weren't served in time to give him the legally required response period. If any of these arguments is valid, the case will be dismissed and the plaintiff may have to start all over again.

Another possible area for questioning by the defendant is venue. The defendant could claim that the location in which the suit was brought does not meet any of the four venue provisions in the small claims rules. If the defendant wins this argument, the case will be dismissed.

There are any number of other "technical" defenses a defendant may try to raise to a small claims action. The defendant might argue that the time period in the statute of limitations has passed and that the plaintiff is consequently barred from filing the action. The defendant also may try to say that the plaintiff has "the wrong guy. I never met this person before in my life."

CONTEST BY THE DEFENDANT

If the defendant wishes to challenge the claims made in the plaintiff's complaint, he must follow a set procedure to properly make this assertion. The yellow copy (Part 2) of the *Notice, Claim, and Summons to Appear for Trial* form that was used to initiate the legal proceeding includes space for the defendant to state the basis for his position that nothing is owed to the plaintiff. The back of the yellow copy of the complaint, which was served on the defendant, gives the defendant three blank lines on which to state why the defendant believes he or she is not liable. This should be done by the defendant in as simple a manner as the corresponding statement made by the plaintiff asserting the original claim.

DEFENDANT'S RESPONSE (Fee for responding is as stated in A below.) I do not owe the Plaintiff(s) or am not responsible to the Plaintiff(s) because: _____

_____

_____

DEFENDANT'S COUNTERCLAIM (If responding or submitting a counterclaim, pay the appropriate filing fees.)
The Plaintiff(s) owe(s) me $_____, which includes penalties, plus interest and costs allowed by law and/or should be ordered to return property, perform a contract or set aside a contract or comply with a restrictive covenant for the following reasons. (Please describe the property being requested).

_____

_____

_____

☐ The amount of my/our counterclaim does not exceed the jurisdictional amount of the Small Claims Court of $7,500.00.
☐ The amount of my/our counterclaim exceeds the jurisdictional amount of the Small Claims Court, but I/we wish to limit the amount that I/we wish to recover from the Plaintiff to $7,500.00.
☐ The amount of my/our counterclaim exceeds the jurisdictional amount of the Small Claims Court, and I/we wish to have the case sent to   ☐ County Court   (only if I/we wish to limit the amount I/we can recover from the plaintiff to $15,000.00)   ☐ District Court (I /we do not wish to limit the amount I/we can recover from the Plaintiff(s)) and will pay the appropriate filing fee. I/we am/are filing a Notice of Removal and paying the appropriate filing fee to the Court at this time.
I am an attorney.   ☐ Yes   ☐ No
I declare under penalty of perjury that this information is true and correct.   _____

                                                                                 Defendant's Address and Telephone Number

                                                                                 _____

_____ _____   _____   _____
Defendant's Signature   Date   Home   Work

A defendant who decides to file a response, or answer, must take this completed form to the small claims clerk's office in the county where the action was filed. The defendant will at this time be assessed a response fee, as set forth below:

Amount of Plaintiff's Claim	Fee
Up to $500	$5.00
$500.01 to $7,500	$15.00

These fees change from time to time and should be checked with the clerk before filing.

Like the filing fees the plaintiff paid when the case was originally filed, these fees are nonrefundable to the defendant. However, if the defendant prevails in the case, the court can order the plaintiff to pay the defendant's response fee, even if no money judgment is granted in favor of the defendant.

While the defendant's method of response bears a certain resemblance to the way the plaintiff filed the original claim, there are important differences between the two. First, the defendant's response does not have to be served on the plaintiff, and, as a practical matter, almost never is. The notion of fairness underlying the need for proper service of the original complaint on the defendant is not present when the defendant files a response. The rationale is that the plaintiff is already aware of the existence of a legal action and the response of the defendant is merely another step in the resolution of that action, and the plaintiff will not suffer unduly if he is not aware of the defendant's response before the trial. The defendant, however, would be in a position to have a default judgment entered against him if he was unaware of the original action, and the rules regarding service of process exist to protect defendants from this possibility.

The plaintiff is free to check periodically with the court in the days leading up to the hearing to see if a response has been filed by the defendant. This is a good precaution for the plaintiff to take, and may provide him with at least some indication of the defendant's position in advance of the hearing.

Often, however, plaintiffs are totally unaware of what stance the defendant is going to take at the hearing until the court date arrives. This is because the deadline for the defendant to file a response is the date of the court hearing. This is an obvious advantage for a defendant, and means that the plaintiff may not know what the other party's defense to the claim will be until the actual hearing. Plaintiffs need to be prepared to counter any possible argument the defendant could make in response to the claim.

DEFENDANT'S COUNTERCLAIM

A further option open to the defendant when a response is filed is the assertion by the defendant of a claim against the plaintiff. This action by the defendant is known as a "counterclaim." This claim need not necessarily arise from the same general facts or incident which is the source of the plaintiff's claim against the defendant. However, if the defendant has a counterclaim which does come from the same source as the plaintiff's original claim, he must raise it now, in this case, or he may not ever sue the plaintiff in any court for an award based on the subject of that counterclaim.

Below the Response on the back of the yellow copy of the *Notice, Claim, and Summons to Appear for Trial* form is space for the defendant to assert a counterclaim. Three blank lines are provided for the defendant to briefly state his position, and space is available to list the amount of the counterclaim. The defendant must complete both the response portion as well as the counterclaim section to properly assert a counterclaim. The defendant must state whether he is an attorney, and must sign and date the form.

DEFENDANT'S RESPONSE (Fee for responding is as stated in A below.) I do not owe the Plaintiff(s) or am not responsible to the Plaintiff(s) because: _____

_____

_____

DEFENDANT'S COUNTERCLAIM (If responding or submitting a counterclaim, pay the appropriate filing fees.)
The Plaintiff(s) owe(s) me $_____, which includes penalties, plus interest and costs allowed by law and/or should be ordered to return property, perform a contract or set aside a contract or comply with a restrictive covenant for the following reasons. (Please describe the property being requested).

_____

_____

_____

☐ The amount of my/our counterclaim does not exceed the jurisdictional amount of the Small Claims Court of $7,500.00.
☐ The amount of my/our counterclaim exceeds the jurisdictional amount of the Small Claims Court, but I/we wish to limit the amount that I/we wish to recover from the Plaintiff to $7,500.00.
☐ The amount of my/our counterclaim exceeds the jurisdictional amount of the Small Claims Court, and I/we wish to have the case sent to ☐ County Court (only if I/we wish to limit the amount I/we can recover from the plaintiff to $15,000.00) ☐ District Court (I /we do not wish to limit the amount I/we can recover from the Plaintiff(s)) and will pay the appropriate filing fee. I/we am/are filing a Notice of Removal and paying the appropriate filing fee to the Court at this time.
I am an attorney. ☐ Yes ☐ No
I declare under penalty of perjury that this information is true and correct. _____

Defendant's Address and Telephone Number

_____

Defendant's Signature   Date   Home   Work

If the defendant is asserting a counterclaim, he must pay a fee based on a different schedule than that used if files only a response. The defendant pays only the response fee OR the counterclaim fee, but not both. The fees for filing a counterclaim are as follows:

Amount of Defendant's Counterclaim	Fee
Up to $500	$10.00
$500.01 to $7,500	$20.00

These fees are also subject to change and should be checked with the clerk of the court before filing.

There is an added complication for defendants here. The law mandating these fees requires that defendants must pay a counterclaim fee based on either the amount of the counterclaim asserted by the defendant or the amount of the original claim by the plaintiff, whichever is greater. For example, if the plaintiff's claim is for $2,200, and the defendant's counterclaim is for $400, the defendant's counterclaim fee is $20, not the $10 as the above table would suggest. This is because the fee for a counterclaim based on the $2,200 the plaintiff is seeking is greater than the counterclaim fee that would result from the $400 the defendant is seeking. If the situation was reversed, with the plaintiff seeking $400 originally and the defendant making a $2,200 counterclaim, the defendant's fee would still be $20, because it is the higher of the two possible fees.

As with the response fees, the counterclaim fees are not refundable to the defendant. But, they may be included in a judgment for costs if the defendant wins at the hearing. There is also no need for service of the defendant's counterclaim on the plaintiff, and the defendant has until the day of the hearing to file the counterclaim. A plaintiff who is hit broadside with a substantial counterclaim by the defendant at the hearing may ask the judge to grant a continuance so the plaintiff may prepare a response to the defendant's counterclaim. While continuances are generally frowned upon in Small Claims Court, one is likely to be allowed in this situation.

Consider the situation in which a plaintiff who is in the home renovation business files suit against a homeowner who would not pay $1,500 due the plaintiff for work done in the defendant's house by the plaintiff. The homeowner believes that the work done by the plaintiff caused damages totaling over $9,000 to his house, and he wants to bring a counterclaim against the plaintiff. What are the defendant's options?

- The defendant must decide between two courses of action. The first is to file the counterclaim for the entire amount in the small claims case brought by the plaintiff. The disadvantage of this option for the defendant is that he can only get a judgment for up to $7,500, the maximum amount a Small Claims Court can award. Any amount above this figure that could have been won is forfeited forever by the defendant. The procedure outlined earlier regarding the defendant's filing of a response in Small Claims Court applies in this situation as well.
- The other approach the defendant may take if he has a

counterclaim of more than $7,500 is to file the counterclaim for the entire amount and simultaneously seek to have the entire matter removed to a higher court, probably the civil division of the County Court. In this scenario, the defendant must file the counterclaim at least seven days before the scheduled small claims trial date. The response filed by the defendant needs to include a written request for the case to be transferred to a different court. The defendant must pay the higher filing fee applicable to a case filed in that other court. When this occurs, the small claims case is discontinued and transferred by the clerk of the Small Claims Court to the clerk of the County Court or District Court to which the case is being moved.

When the case reaches the County Court or District Court, the relaxed rules of court procedure which govern Small Claims Court no longer apply. The plaintiff, in a case in which the defendant has transferred the case in this manner, should consider obtaining the services of an attorney.

The law of Small Claims Court includes a warning to defendants who might want to pursue this course of action. If the County or District Court, which receives a case transferred from Small Claims Court by a defendant based on a counterclaim exceeding $7,500, subsequently determines that the plaintiff is entitled to a judgment against the defendant and that the counterclaim was filed solely to defeat the dollar amount limit of the Small Claims Court, and was without merit, the County or District Court can also award the plaintiff costs, including reasonable attorney fees, incurred by the plaintiff in the handling of the case in the new court. Any defendant in a small claims case should be mindful of this possibility before filing a counterclaim which exceeds the maximum amount allowable in Small Claims Court.

Small Claims Court, _____ County, Colorado
Court Address:

PLAINTIFF(S): _____

Address: _____

City/State/Zip: _____

Phone: Home _____ Work _____

v.

DEFENDANT(S): _____

Address: _____

City/State/Zip: _____

▲ **COURT USE ONLY** ▲

Phone: Home _____ Work _____

Case Number:

Attorney or Party Without Attorney (Name and Address):

Phone Number: E-mail:

FAX Number: Atty. Reg. #:   Division: Courtroom:

NOTICE OF REMOVAL

I, _____, Defendant(s) have/has requested that this case be removed to ☐ County Court or ☐ District Court pursuant to C.R.C.P. 508(c)(2), on the grounds that the counterclaim in this action exceeds the jurisdictional limits of the Small Claims Court.

Date: _____   _____
                                       Signature of Defendant or Defendant's Attorney

NOTICE TO PLAINTIFF(S)/DEFENDANT(S):

This Small Claims case is removed to ☐ County Court or ☐ District Court. Do not appear in Small Claims Court on the date shown on the Notice, Claim and Summons to Appear for Trial.

☐ Your new case number is _____.
☐ The new Court date is _____ at (time) _____.
☐ See attached Court notice.

Date: _____   _____
                                       Clerk of Court/Deputy Clerk

CERTIFICATE OF MAILING

I hereby certify that on (date) _____, I mailed a true and correct copy of the NOTICE OF REMOVAL, by placing it in the United States Mail, postage pre-paid to the parties at the addresses listed above.

_____
Clerk of Court/Deputy Clerk

JDF 251 R9/01 NOTICE OF REMOVAL

DEFENDANT'S RIGHT TO LEGAL REPRESENTATION

The philosophy which underlies the whole notion of Small Claims Court is that there should be a forum for parties to resolve disputes without the need for incurring the expense of retaining attorneys. At the same time, there is the principle that any party sued in court should have the right to be represented by legal counsel if that party so chooses. The defendant may choose to exercise this option by filing a *Notice of Representation by Attorney* with the Court. This form must be filed at least seven days before the first scheduled trial date. If the form is not filed before this deadline, neither party may be represented by an attorney in the case.

If the Notice is filed on time, the Court will then notify you of this fact and advise you that you have the right to hire your own attorney. A plaintiff in this situation must now decide whether to retain the services of an attorney. This may be a hard notion to accept, given that the plaintiff filed the case in Small Claims Court just so hiring an attorney would not be necessary. There is no requirement that the plaintiff have an attorney, even if the defendant will have one.

Make your decision based on factors such as the amount of money at stake, the complexity of the case, the strength of your evidence, and your willingness to prepare and practice. Consider also that even if one or both parties are represented by lawyers, the trial will proceed on the originally scheduled date under the more relaxed rules of the Small Claims Court rather than the more formal procedures which usually exist in cases where both parties are represented by attorneys. This means that a plaintiff who feels that he has a good case and feels prepared and confident may consider going without formal legal representation.

Small Claims Court, _____ County, Colorado

Court Address:

PLAINTIFF(S): _____

Address: _____

City/State/Zip: _____

Phone: Home _____ Work _____

v.

DEFENDANT(S): _____

Address: _____

City/State/Zip: _____

Phone: Home _____ Work _____

Attorney or Party Without Attorney (Name and Address):

Phone Number: E-mail:

FAX Number: Atty. Reg. #:

▲ COURT USE ONLY ▲

Case Number:

Division: Courtroom:

NOTICE OF REPRESENTATION BY ATTORNEY

TO THE COURT AND TO THE PLAINTIFF(S) NAMED ABOVE:

Please take notice that Defendant(s) _____,
will be represented by: _____,
an attorney at the trial of the above-captioned matter.
Plaintiff(s) may now be represented by an attorney if Plaintiff(s) wishes. **However, it is not required that Paintiff(s) be represented by an attorney.**

Please further take notice that this Notice of Representation by Attorney must be filed with the court at least seven days **prior** to the first scheduled trial date in this matter. If not filed at least seven days **prior** to the first scheduled trial date, the Court shall strike this notice and neither party may be represented by an attorney at the trial.

NOTE: Defendant(s) must make payment of the filing fee required for defendant's answer (and counterclaim, if any is anticipated) at the time of the filing of the Notice of Representation by Attorney.

_____   _____
Defendant's Signature   Date   Attorney's Signature   Date

CERTIFICATE OF MAILING

I hereby certify on (date) _____ the original of this document was filed with the Court;
and a true a accurate copy of the NOTICE OF REPRESENTATION BY ATTORNEY was served on the Plaintiff(s) by
placing it in the United States Mail, postage pre-paid at the address(es) listed above.

Date: _____

_____
Defendant/Attorney

JDF 256 9/01 NOTICE OF REPRESENTATION BY ATTORNEY

SAM'S CASE

Sam contacted the court to see if any response had been filed by Bob. The court clerk searched the case file and told Sam that a response and a counterclaim had been filed by the defendant on September 14th.

Sam could not believe Bob had filed a counterclaim. He went to the Small Claims Court the next day to read the contents of Bob's counterclaim. What he saw was this:

DEFENDANT'S RESPONSE (Fee for responding is as stated in A below.) I do not owe the Plaintiff(s) or am not responsible to the Plaintiff(s) because: ___The trees Mr. Grant planted at my house were defective. They have begun to die and are turning brown, despite my efforts to keep them alive.

DEFENDANT'S COUNTERCLAIM (If responding or submitting a counterclaim, pay the appropriate filing fees.)
The Plaintiff(s) owe(s) me $___1,000.00___, which includes penalties, plus interest and costs allowed by law and/or should be ordered to return property, perform a contract or set aside a contract or comply with a restrictive covenant for the following reasons. (Please describe the property being requested).
I paid the plaintiff this money for trees which turned out to be defective. Mr. Grant said they were guaranteed for one year.

☐ The amount of my/our counterclaim does not exceed the jurisdictional amount of the Small Claims Court of $7,500.00.
☐ The amount of my/our counterclaim exceeds the jurisdictional amount of the Small Claims Court, but I/we wish to limit the amount that I/we wish to recover from the Plaintiff to $7,500.00.
☐ The amount of my/our counterclaim exceeds the jurisdictional amount of the Small Claims Court, and I/we wish to have the case sent to ☐ County Court (only if I/we wish to limit the amount I/we can recover from the plaintiff to $15,000.00) ☐ District Court (I /we do not wish to limit the amount I/we can recover from the Plaintiff(s)) and will pay the appropriate filing fee. I/we am/are filing a Notice of Removal and paying the appropriate filing fee to the Court at this time.
I am an attorney. ☐ Yes ☐ No
I declare under penalty of perjury that this information is true and correct.

Bob Lee   9-13-02
Defendant's Signature   Date

1591 South Dahlia Street
Defendant's Address and Telephone Number
Denver, Colorado 80224
303-555-3333
Home   Work

Sam could not imagine what Bob was talking about. There was no way those trees were dead. They were perfectly healthy when Sam had picked them up from the nursery and brought them to Bob's house.

What was Bob trying to pull here, Sam wondered.

No Action by the Defendant

The final course of action the defendant may take in response to a case filed against him in Small Claims Court is ... nothing. There is no absolute requirement that the defendant file a response, much less a counterclaim. The defendant will not be arrested or sought out by the court. However, the defendant will be vulnerable to the possibility of a default judgment if no answer is filed to the complaint.

As the plaintiff, you need to be cautious even if it looks as though the defendant will file no response. You must proceed to prepare for the court hearing without regard to whether the defendant files a response. Remember, the defendant has until the day of the hearing to file a response, so you may not find out about it until you stroll into the courtroom and see the defendant. Even if you have not heard from the defendant by the night before the hearing, it is never safe to assume that you will win the case by default.

Let's turn to preparation for the court hearing.

Witness   Photos   Subpoenas   Demand Letter

Chapter 6: Preparing for the Court Hearing

REVIEWING YOUR CASE

After you, the plaintiff, have filed your small claims case and successfully served the defendant with a copy of the complaint, it is time to begin preparing for your upcoming court date. You should start these preparations without regard to the possible reaction of the defendant. You will still have to prove your case to the court no matter what the defendant's response.

Your first task is to look at the big picture. Consider what information will convince a person who knows nothing about you, the defendant, or your dispute, that the defendant really does owe you money. What events, transactions, or incidents led to a situation in which the defendant is liable to you and you have suffered damages? What documents, pictures, witnesses, or other types of information can be used as evidence to help you prove your case to a judge?

Begin with your demand letter. Remember that one of the purposes of this letter was to provide you with a written account of the facts of the dispute. You can now draw on it to see what types of information will be most helpful in proving your case to a neutral third party—the judge.

Draft an outline of the case. Start with the underlying incident that began the dispute. Then put in writing the reasons why you think the defendant is liable to you. Continue with an accounting of your damages, and how you calculated the dollar amount stated in your claim. Then list any evidence you have in your possession or need to get from someone else that could help you prove the case. Next name any witnesses who saw the incident or who have special knowledge which can further your explanation of the case. End the outline with a concluding statement which summarizes your case.

The ideal outcome of this exercise is to allow you to be in a situation where you can clearly and succinctly explain your case to someone totally unfamiliar with it, with the result that it is obvious that the defendant owes you the amount of your claim. The desired product is a case outline which presents the facts in an organized and understandable way. This will help you present your case to the judge more effectively, and will make it easier for the judge to rule in your favor.

Compiling your case outline will force you to determine what is necessary to prove the claim you stated in your complaint. It should also help you identify things that are not vital to your case. This is the time to be as objective as you possibly can. You must strive to eliminate all those items which are really not relevant to its resolution.

Do not include:
- That the defendant was rude to you, or that he used profanity. Leave out the opinions of your friends and family.
- That you know that the defendant also wronged someone else in a similar manner. These types of irrelevant details and emotions should not be a part of your case outline, nor should they be a part of your case presentation in court. Stick to the facts.

You may need to do some research to provide yourself with a stronger base of knowledge regarding the subject of your case. You know the defendant's repairs to your car were inadequate, but can you explain why? A book on the subject, such as an auto mechanics manual, might be helpful. Reading the law relating to the subject of the case will help you become more familiar with the issues the judge will have to consider. While it is not necessary to become an expert in the field your case pertains to, you must be knowledgeable enough to explain your claim and why the defendant owes you money. If you can't do this, consider asking an expert to coach you or to serve as a witness for you.

WRITTEN OR PRINTED EVIDENCE

Depending on the nature of your case, the evidence you will need to prove your position in court may or may not be readily apparent. A case involving the defendant's failure to pay on a promissory note will be proven through the production of the note signed by the defendant. Instances involving defective products or poor workmanship will probably require a receipt, contract, or canceled checks showing payment to the defendant. In cases involving repairs necessitated by damages caused by the defendant, you will need estimates from qualified repair firms, as well as any receipts or canceled checks you may have as a result of having repairs made.

Besides collecting the more obvious papers associated with your case, such as bills, receipts, and canceled checks, try thinking of how to use other printed matter in creative ways to help you with your case. If you were drawn to buy something by a newspaper advertisement, bought the product, but later found it was not what you were expecting, track down a copy of that newspaper ad. It may give the judge grounds to rule that certain promises were made by the defendant in the advertisement, but the promises were not kept, and you are now entitled to compensation. This can be especially helpful if you have had a bad experience buying a used car from a private individual based on a newspaper classified ad. The same can be true in the case of a defendant making promises about providing a service, who later does not abide by these promises and thinks he can get away with it because he does not think you can prove that the promises were ever made.

There are other written pieces of evidence which can prove useful in certain types of cases. In a motor vehicle fender-bender case, you should consider obtaining a copy of the police accident report, if one was completed. If, after reading the report, you think it is helpful to your case, include it as part of your package of evidence.

DIAGRAMS

Diagrams you create can assist the judge in determining the outcome of your case. The need for a diagram can be paramount in a car accident case. Help the judge visualize what occurred by creating a diagram on a large piece of hard paper or cardboard which recreates the intersection in question with straight lines, bright colors, and local landmarks. The diagram need not be absolutely professional looking, but it must be accurate. Even though you, an interested party, created this piece of evidence yourself, the court will still probably allow it as evidence, as long as there are no glaring mistakes in it. Just remember that you will be called upon to explain the diagram and how it is relevant to the case.

Diagrams can also be instructive in cases involving home renovations and landscaping. If a contractor mistakenly put a bedroom where a second bathroom was supposed to be, a diagram detailing the interior layout of the plaintiff's home might be called for. Similarly, if a landscaping contractor places a row of lilac bushes where a small pond was supposed to go, a diagram showing this can easily be prepared.

PICTURES

While documentary evidence can provide an important foundation for proving your case, some cases need more. In these cases, photographs can often serve to educate the judge about your position in the dispute.

An example of a case which would benefit from photographic evidence is a minor auto accident case. A few pictures showing the accident scene, the placement of your vehicle, and close-ups of the actual damage to your car could be of interest to the judge. Also of interest, but not as easy to get, would be similar shots of the defendant's vehicle. If it is possible to get such pictures without trespassing, by all means try to do so.

The same goes for cases involving home remodeling projects gone bad. Pictures showing the shoddy work of a contractor can help the judge see the point you are trying to make. In fact, any case involving damage to physical property can be assisted by the inclusion of photos illustrating the damage.

Pictures can be taken by a Polaroid or any other type of camera which produces clear pictures. Professional quality photographs are not required. Be sure to date the back of the pictures and to write a short description of what the photo shows.

PHYSICAL EVIDENCE

While it is not practical to haul a damaged car into a courtroom, it is reasonable to bring other items which have been damaged or are defective to the court hearing. If your case involves such an item, consider bringing it with you.

Examples of the types of cases where this might work include those which are brought by customers of a dry cleaning establishment who feel their garments were damaged by the cleaners. You should bring the damaged clothing item to the hearing, along with any relevant paperwork, such as the receipt or a canceled check, and even the receipt showing the purchase price of the garment. It is important to remember, however, that merely producing such an item is not enough to win a case. You must also prove to the judge that the defendant is liable for the damage, and what the extent of the damage is.

Another instance where bringing the item in question to the court hearing may be helpful is the situation where you purchased a product which later proved to be defective. You should bring the item to the court hearing to show the judge that it does not work. The defendant may still argue that it was your fault, that it was working when it was sold, or that it was sold without any warranty, and that he is not liable.

WITNESSES

Some of the most effective evidence you can present in a small claims case is testimony from a witness who was present at the incident or who later saw and assessed damage to your property. You will still have to prove your case to the judge, but words from a witness who was there or who can competently comment on the damage you have sustained can bolster the presentation of your case.

Witnesses are not required in a small claims case. Many cases, such as those based solely on documentary evidence such as a promissory note signed by the defendant, really do not need witnesses to testify as to the defendant's signature. Rather, use witnesses when they can enhance your case and provide information to the court that you cannot, or when they corroborate testimony which backs up your claim.

One type of witness is the person who may have been present at the time of the incident which resulted in your damage. This can include eyewitnesses to a car accident, people who were present when the defendant made certain promises, or someone who saw your house after the defendant damaged it. It does not include people who heard about the accident, or talked to someone about it later, or who have encountered similar treatment from the defendant in the past. The person must be a first-hand witness to some aspect of the case.

Another type of witness is that person who has seen the damage and is able to assess the extent of the damage and its cause based on that person's knowledge and special training in a relevant field of expertise. Such a person can often provide both an appraisal of the damage and an estimate of the cost of repairs. For example, you can bring in an automobile mechanic as a witness to testify that the repairs performed by the defendant were not those the plaintiff paid for, or a plumber to say that the renovation work done by the defendant contractor necessitates $1,000 worth of repairs to the plaintiff's house. A defendant, in turn, could use a witness who will say that the quality of work done by the defendant is customary for the industry in a certain situation. The expert witness must be familiar with your case, and must have actually examined the damage or the damaged item before he or she can testify about it. It is not enough that you described the damage to this person, and hope he says something like "sounds like you need a new engine, and that'll cost you $3,000." This type of testimony is not permissible.

Another kind of testimony the court does not want to hear is that related to someone's character. It is not helpful to the court to have a plaintiff parade his three best friends before the judge saying what a great guy the plaintiff is. Also not really helpful is testimony from someone you have dealt with before stating that the plaintiff always does a good job and is an honorable person. That witness has no direct knowledge of the case in dispute and can offer no testimony helpful to the court. Likewise, it is not a good idea to bring in a witness to testify about what a bad person the defendant is and how that witness had a bad experience with the defendant.

You may also bring in the testimony of witnesses in the form of a letter to you from that witness outlining what he or she would have said at the court hearing. Be aware, however, that a live witness will provide far better testimony for you than any letter from that person. The judge will have the chance to observe the witness and ask questions. You can get information from this witness to the court that may not be included in the letter. Only use a written statement by a witness if you cannot get him or her to appear at the trial.

After you have determined what witnesses can be helpful to you, approach them to see if they would be willing to testify for you. Be sure each witness is available on the date and at the time of the court hearing. Also go over with each witness what points you want him or her to make at the court hearing. Have an eyewitness tell where she was and how she came to be in a position to witness the incident. Make sure an expert witness or appraiser begins her testimony by stating information about her credentials in the relevant field. Too often, witnesses will testify about things you were not expecting to hear about at the trial. Be sure you know what your witness is going to say ahead of time.

You must remember that your witnesses are your responsibility. You need to make sure they know where to appear, when to appear, as well as what they are expected to say. Be certain that they know exactly where the court is, and how to get there. You may want to arrange to pick them up on the day of the hearing, or arrange for a taxi to pick them up, if necessary. If your witnesses do not show up, expect no sympathy from the court. The case will more than likely continue without them.

SUBPEONAS

The rules of Small Claims Court provide both the plaintiff and defendant a mechanism by which they can compel the testimony of witnesses or the production of documents from those who are unwilling to cooperate. This is done through the use of subpoenas which compel people who are not parties to the case to testify or bring documents to your court hearing.

You can use subpoenas on either those who are quite willing to testify for you or those who are not. Serving a subpoena on a cooperative witness gives her formal notice of the time and place of the court hearing. It may also entitle her to witness fees. Most importantly, it can be helpful if the witness must be away from work. An employer is more likely to be persuaded to let the witness be gone from the job when presented with a formal subpoena than a verbal request from the witness like, "I have to go testify in a small claims case today. Can I have the morning off?"

Although it is legally permissible, you should have a very good reason before you serve a subpoena on a party unwilling to testify in your small claims case. Human nature dictates that a person forced into testifying in court by you may not be inclined to give testimony that favors your position. However, there are cases where this is necessary, and you can issue a subpoena to a witness by following the correct procedure.

You can tell the court clerk when you file your initial complaint that you wish to serve a subpoena. You can also have a subpoena issued after you have filed. The clerk will provide you with a Subpoena form, JDF 254. The form offers you two choices, one for a regular *Subpoena,* and another for a *Subpoena to Produce.* You need to check one of these boxes when you complete the form, depending on whether you are asking the person to testify or asking them to testify and bring documents relating to the case.

Mark the box *Subpoena* if you want a witness to testify at your trial. Complete the remainder of the top half of the form, including the person's name, and the date and location of the trial, and your name as the party for whom the witness will testify. Also list the names of all parties named as plaintiffs and defendants in the action. Do not complete the three blank lines above the court clerk's signature line. Return the form to the court clerk for his or her signature.

If you want a party to testify *and* bring some sort of record or document to the trial, check the box marked *Subpoena to Produce.* This form will compel the witness to come testify at the trial and produce the written documentation you are seeking. Complete the form as described above, but this time put the name or type of documents you are requesting on the three lines above the clerk's signature line. It may be that you know what sort of document you need, but are unsure who in a large business actually has the records. In this case, you may just put "Custodian of Records" instead of a person's name in the space

Small Claims Court, _____ County, Colorado

Court Address:

PLAINTIFF(S): _____

Address: _____

City/State/Zip: _____

Phone: Home _____ Work _____

v.

DEFENDANT(S): _____

Address: _____

City/State/Zip: _____

Phone: Home _____ Work _____

▲ **COURT USE ONLY** ▲

Case Number:

Division: Courtroom:

☐ SUBPOENA   OR   ☐ SUBPOENA TO PRODUCE

TO: _____

You are ordered to attend and give testimony in the Small Claims Division of _____
County Court at (location) _____ on
(date) _____, at (time) _____, as a witness for _____
_____ in an action between _____ Plaintiff(s),
and _____ Defendant(s), and also to produce at this time and place (if applicable):
_____
_____
_____ now in your control.

Date: _____   _____
                                             Clerk of Court/Deputy Clerk

RETURN OF SERVICE

State of _____

County _____

I declare under oath that I served this Subpoena or Subpoena To Produce on _____
in _____ County on (date) _____, at (time) _____,
at the following location: _____
and that I tendered witness(es) fees and mileage to _____
☐ by (state manner of service) _____
_____.

☐ I am over the age of 18 years and am not interested in nor a party to this case.

Subscribed and affirmed, or sworn to before me in the
County of _____,
State of _____, this _____
day of _____, 20 _____.

My commission expires: _____

_____   _____
Name   Date

☐ Private process server
☐ Sheriff, _____ County
Fee $ _____   Mileage $ _____

_____
Notary Public

JDF 254   R9/01   SUBPOENA OR SUBPOENA TO PRODUCE

on the form where it indicates upon whom the subpoena is to be served. The best way to state this is to also include the business name and address on this line.

Once the subpoena form has been completed and signed by the court clerk, you must have it personally served on the defendant as set out in the rules of service of legal process. Certified mail is not an option for serving a subpoena. Have the sheriff or a private process server do this for you, and have him complete the Return of Service portion of the form. They will also charge you a service fee.

At this time, you will also have to pay the witness fee. These are usually nominal, and include a base fee—around $3— plus a mileage charge of fifteen cents per mile one way from the witness' residence to the court. Of course, you may not have any idea where the witness lives and thus no way to compute the correct mileage charge. Do the calculation based on a liberal estimation of the distance. Then add the two amounts and attach a check for this final figure to the subpoena when you give it to the process server.

Service of the subpoena and the accompanying witness fee must be accomplished no later than 48 hours before the court hearing. Allow substantially more time than this if you are serious about the subpoena.

A witness who has been served with the subpoena but does not appear at the hearing can be charged with contempt of court, but it is extremely unlikely that this person will be put in jail. It is also quite unlikely that you will be granted a continuance. Try not to rely on making your case via the testimony of subpoenaed witnesses. As noted earlier, they, too, are your responsibility.

SAM'S CASE

Sam reviewed the demand letter he had sent Bob in July. He drafted a case outline detailing how he would explain to the judge that Bob was liable to him for $1,000. The outline began with a recitation of the way in which he and Bob had gotten together and come to an agreement for Sam to plant trees in Bob's yard, and that the price they agreed on for the job was $2,000, and that Bob had paid Sam a deposit of $1,000 at that time. The outline went on to note that Sam had bought the trees from a local nursery, delivered them to Bob's house, and planted the trees on May 24.

Sam next put in his outline that he had left an invoice at Bob's home for the remaining $1,000, but had not received Bob's payment. Sam included mention of his call to Bob to see what was going on, and Bob's response that indicated he could not pay the rest of the money to Sam. Sam made reference to the demand letter that he had sent to Bob, and that no reply to it was ever received by Sam. The outline concluded by stating that to date, Sam had still not been paid by Bob.

Sam next considered what pieces of evidence would help him prove his case. Sam wanted to kick himself when he realized there was no written contract. However, he did have a copy of the invoice that he had left at Bob's house, which showed the delivery and planting of the trees as well as the fact that Bob was given credit for having paid half in advance and still owed Sam $1,000. This invoice certainly implied the existence of a business arrangement between himself and Bob. Sam also contacted his bank to get a copy of the check that Bob had used to pay him, which had later been deposited in Sam's business bank account. This, too, could show that there was a contract for these trees as Sam was claiming.

Sam was concerned about how to defend against Bob's counterclaim that the trees Sam had planted were dead or dying. Sam had to see for himself, so he went to Bob's house during the day when he presumed Bob was away at work. Fortunately, the trees were clearly visible over a low split rail fence. Being careful not to trespass on Bob's property, Sam surveyed the trees from the sidewalk. They were still where Sam had planted them more than three months ago. More importantly, they appeared to be not only alive, but also thriving. Sam ran back to his pickup and got his camera. He began taking pictures of the trees from several different angles, always making sure he stayed off Bob's property.

He next stopped by a one-hour photo store and got the pictures developed. Sam believed they clearly showed that the trees were alive and well in Bob's backyard. He chose the five best photos, and dated them and wrote a brief description of what was in each picture on the back of each shot.

While Sam was pleased with the results of the photographs, he wanted more evidence that the trees he planted at Bob's house were healthy. He decided to approach George Thomas, the owner of the nursery where Sam had bought the trees. George had helped Sam choose the trees and had even assisted in the loading of the trees into Sam's truck on the same day Sam had planted the trees at Bob's. George could speak to the good condition of the trees.

George agreed to testify for Sam, because he considered Sam a friend as well as one of his best customers. They agreed that Sam would pick up George at the nursery at 9 a.m. on the day of the hearing.

Sam next organized his presentation for the court hearing. He revised his case outline to include the photos and George's testimony. He also practiced what he was going to say to the judge and made sure he got plenty of sleep the night before the court hearing.

PULLING IT ALL TOGETHER

After you have obtained all the documents, records, physical evidence, and witnesses you will need for your case, review your case outline. See if you need to add or drop anything from it based on how your collection of evidence has gone. Make any needed revisions. Also, be sure to make four copies of any papers, receipts, estimates, police reports, or other documents you will need. This will allow you to keep the original while allowing for you, the defendant, the judge, and a witness to review the copies at the trial. Make sure you still have the Certificate of Personal Service, unless service by certified mail was successful.

Now that your background material has been gathered, you are ready to face the big day.

Chapter 7: Tips for Common Cases

You now know how to initiate a small claims court action, determine liability and file the case. You know how to determine venue and when a court holds small claims hearings. You are familiar with the preparation of evidence and witnesses, and how to issue a subpoena.

The information in this book thus far is applicable to almost every kind of case in Small Claims Court. Now let's touch on some specifics of some of the most common cases.

WHEN SOMEONE OWES YOU MONEY

One of the most common case types in Small Claims Court involves disputes over money owed. These cases can take many forms. The simplest case deals with someone going back on a promise to pay another party in return for goods or services. Some instances involve bad checks, or checks which were later the subject of a stop payment order made by the buyer. Others are based on promissory notes or contracts.

The general rule for these cases is that the more paperwork there is, the easier it is to prove and win the case. Remember, to prevail in a case like this, you need to show two things. First, you have to prove that the other party really did owe you money pursuant to some type of agreement, and, second, that you have not been paid based on the terms of the agreement.

You have to prove to the court that there was an agreement which created a duty to pay on the part of the defendant. This is most easily shown with a promissory note, a returned check, or a written contract. Each of these is merely a vehicle which puts on paper one party's promise to pay money to another. The mere existence of one of these items containing a valid signature from the defendant is usually enough to establish the duty to pay.

Obtaining a money judgment is more difficult in cases in which there is no written proof of an agreement. Without a written agreement, you must use other evidence to try to infer the existence of the agreement. This can include correspondence you have received from the other party, including a response to your demand letter. If no written evidence exists, you must rely on the actions of the parties to prove that there really is an agreement. You will need to show that you performed certain tasks only because there was an agreement in place between you and the other party. You need to be able to describe the situation in such a way as to make the judge believe that the only reasonable conclusion she can reach is that there was a binding agreement. A witness who heard you and the other party reach a verbal agreement can be helpful.

Non-payment can be shown relatively simply. If you have no written records, merely allege that you have not received your money. This puts the onus on the other party to prove that payment was made. A bounced check is certainly a good indication that payment was not made. A business suing on a debt may have more detailed payment records. By all means bring these records to court or bring the bookkeeper as a witness.

Don't forget to note any relevant information from whatever written materials you have in case that can help you in the collection process. Even a bad check contains good information about where a debtor banks, as well as addresses and phone numbers. Most contracts and accompanying credit applications are great sources for this data as well.

WHEN YOU OWE BUT DON'T THINK
YOU SHOULD HAVE TO PAY — OR,
"I WANT MY MONEY BACK!"

This category of case is the flip side of those discussed in the previous section. In this situation, there's no argument about whether an agreement was ever in place. There was, but one party did not live up to its end of the bargain because of faulty goods or services delivered. "This," says the buyer, "releases me from my duty to pay the seller."

This situation usually arises in one of two ways. The first is in cases like those discussed in the previous section, in which the buyer is the defendant being sued for non-payment by the seller. The other finds the buyer as the plaintiff suing the seller to recover payments made for merchandise or services which the plaintiff feels did not live up to the agreement.

Buyers can bring or defend against cases like this based on either an express written warranty provided by the seller, on verbal statements made by the seller or a representative of the seller, or on the general notion that a product is implicitly warranted to perform the purpose for which it is intended. Having the warranty in writing is generally a good thing, because it specifically binds the seller. However, some also limit the actions of the buyer. For example, many warranties state that the product in question may not be put to a commercial use, or that the warranty is no longer effective if the product is misused by the purchaser. You may also be required to make the seller aware of the problem before filing suit. Be sure to review any written warranties carefully if you need to sue or defend in such a case.

As in other scenarios, some cases are easier to prove than others. If you bought a piece of electronic equipment that came with a 90 day warranty, and it gives out after only a week, you have a very strong case. Always contact the seller first and ask for a replacement item or a refund. Legal action should be taken only when the merchant fails to honor its written warranty within a reasonable time. Sue for whatever amount you have paid for the item thus far. Bring all paperwork, including the receipt showing the purchase price and the warranty, to the court hearing. If possible, bring the item, too.

There are other situations in which getting your money back may be a more difficult task. These cases often involve products which do work, but maybe not quite in the way you imagined, or not as well as they were supposed to. To make your case in these instances, you may have to rely on what you were told by a salesperson. If you have a witness who also heard what the salesperson said, have that person testify. You can also put into evidence newspaper advertisements which feature additional promises made by the seller about a product. Anything which even infers that a representation was made about a product is helpful here.

Finally, there are situations in which you may feel you have the right to a refund, but, legally, you do not. Say your dream is to look out your window and watch a row of lilacs bloom next spring, so you order and pay for a dozen lilac bushes to be planted in your backyard by a local nursery. Only after they've been firmly rooted in the ground do you realize that the plants are years away from flowering. In your mind, you ordered bushes that would bloom every April from now on. But because you were not specific in your order, and because the nursery made no representations about the lilacs, the agreement has been met by the seller. About the only thing you could rely on would be a general guarantee of satisfaction given by the seller, such as "your satisfaction or your money back." The lesson here is to know what you're buying before you pay for it.

Whatever the case, remember that you will have to do more than tell the court that you didn't like the product, or that it doesn't work. You will need to show the court the source of your dissatisfaction, and why the defect or inadequacy is covered by your agreement with the seller before a court will rule that you are excused from paying the seller. Also, remember to bring the original copy of the warranty or agreement to court with you. You can also use cancelled checks or receipts to indicate what you've paid so far.

As with any case involving a business, buyers must make sure to bring suit against the proper defendant. Be certain that you have the business name and address listed correctly, and do not forget to check with the Secretary of State's office to see if the business is incorporated and has a registered agent for the service of process.

SECURITY DEPOSIT CASES

Colorado law has several specific provisions which deal with security deposits given by tenants to landlords when rental agreements are made between these two parties. It has been said that this section of the law is the only one which favors tenants.

A landlord must return a security deposit to the tenant within one month after the termination of a lease or the surrender of the premises. The lease can specify a longer period, but this period can't exceed 60 days. The provisions regarding the return of the security deposit may not be waived by the tenant in the lease, or in any other written or verbal agreement.

Landlords who keep even a portion of the security deposit must provide the tenant with a written statement which sets out, in detail, exactly what amounts have been retained and why. Portions of a security deposit may be kept by the landlord for non-payment of rent or utility charges, abandonment of the property, repair work, and cleaning. Costs assessed as "normal wear and tear" may not be charged to a tenant's security deposit. If the landlord does not deliver the refund and/or a statement accounting for the retained portions of the security deposit within the required time, the landlord loses all right to withhold any portion of the security deposit.

As noted in chapter two, a landlord who does not return the deposit within the required time may be liable for triple damages. To get triple damages, a tenant must give the landlord notice that the tenant intends to file a legal action regarding the security deposit. This notice, in writing, must be received by the landlord at least seven days prior to the filing of a court case. The tenant should send such a notice via certified mail, return receipt requested, to ensure proof to the Small Claims Court that the notice was properly delivered.

The suit should claim damages in an amount equal to three times the amount of the security deposit which has not been returned. Be sure to lessen your claim by any amount the landlord may have refunded you.

The landlord has the burden of showing why it was proper to retain part or all of the security deposit. While this rule may seem to make it easier for a tenant to win, this advantage can be offset by the fact that a landlord may have been through dozens of similar cases in the past, while a typical tenant may have never been to Small Claims Court.

Tenants must be able to show that they have lived up to their end of the lease. Leaving the apartment clean is vital, as is collecting evidence which clearly shows it. Photographs, receipts for cleaning services, and even friends and neighbors who saw the place when you moved out can help your case. If the landlord gave you a checklist which showed the condition of the property when you moved in, bring this to the hearing as evidence that you didn't cause the problems.

Landlords may respond with cleaning bills of their own, as well as with witnesses who will testify about how dirty the property was after you moved out. Some landlords will call on the new tenant, who may be less impressed with your efforts to beautify the place than you are.

Be sure to sue and serve the right defendants. Check your lease to get the correct address of the property's owner. If you are not sure who is the manager and who is the owner, sue both and let them sort it out.

The threat of triple damages compels many landlords to settle this type of case. A little preparation and determination can help you get your money returned.

SUITS BY LANDLORDS

Landlords may find themselves in situations which require them to file an action in Small Claims Court against a tenant. Probably the most common reason for these actions is the failure of a tenant to pay the rent. This can occur both when the tenant remains in the property or when the tenant skips out before the expiration of the lease. Landlords may bring actions in Small Claims Court seeking money damages based on the amount of rent which remains unpaid. They may not, however, bring an action in Small Claims Court seeking to evict the tenant for non-payment of rent.

If the tenant has moved out of the property, there is a better than even chance that the tenant will not appear at the hearing in Small Claims Court. The landlord can prevail by merely showing a copy of the lease and alleging that the rent remains unpaid for certain periods covered by the lease. Be sure to bring to court any records which show that the rent was not paid.

A tenant who remains in the property may claim that, for some reason, the property is "uninhabitable," thus excusing the tenant from paying rent until the landlord fixes the problem. Colorado law, with one exception, does not recognize this defense. Tenants must continue to pay rent regardless, and can be sued if they fail to do so.

The exception to this rule concerns gas appliances. If a tenant is informed by a gas company service person of a hazardous condition, the tenant must immediately notify the landlord in writing. The landlord then has 72 hours to make repairs. Failure to do so means the lease is null and void, and the tenant may vacate the property without any further responsibility to pay the rent. The tenant can then demand return of the security deposit, and the landlord has another 72 hours to comply. If this time passes without the return of the security deposit and/ or a retention statement, the tenant is entitled to double the amount of the deposit. This latter three-day period excludes Saturdays, Sundays, and holidays.

Landlords may also sue tenants for physical damage to property for which the costs of repairs exceed the amount of the security deposit. Landlords must show that the tenant was responsible for the damage, and be able to prove the dollar amount of the damages. Estimates of, or receipts for, repairs and cleaning work well in this situation.

Note that the amount a landlord may sue for can be offset by the landlord's duty to mitigate the damages caused by a tenant, either via property damage or unpaid rent. For example, when a tenant leaves a property before a lease has expired, the landlord must attempt to rent the property to someone else. A landlord must also make an effort to stop any ongoing damage, even if the tenant was the original source of that damage. If a tenant caused a water pipe to spring a leak, a landlord must see that the leak is fixed within a reasonable time after the landlord becomes aware of it. The landlord can't sit back and let the damages mount and then sue the tenant for the entire amount. Likewise, if the landlord is successful in renting a tenant's property to someone else, the landlord's claim against the tenant would be reduced by the amount of rent the landlord was receiving from the new tenant.

Landlords should use the materials at their disposal to

assist them in collection efforts. The information on a rental application can be an invaluable source of data regarding the debtor's job and assets. The information found on the tenant's earlier rent checks, such as account numbers and bank locations, can give landlords a leg up in pursuing a wage garnishment or a bank garnishment against the tenant.

Landlords who are interested in pursuing eviction actions against tenants will find a book entitled *Landlord & Tenant Guide to Colorado Evictions*, Second Edition, authored by Victor M. Grimm and published by Bradford Publishing Company of Denver, to be an excellent source of information about the eviction process.

UNPAID WAGES

You show up Friday at the donut shop where you work, even though you're not scheduled to work that day. Why? Because it's payday, and you need your paycheck to make it through the weekend. Your boss, the owner of the shop, has your check ready when you stop in. A quick trip to the bank gives you some money in both your account and your pocket.

The following Tuesday brings bad news, however. After working your shift at the donut shop, you return home to find a letter from your bank in the mailbox. The notice tells you that the check you deposited on Friday is not backed up by sufficient funds to cover the amount of the check. The amount of money in your account, sadly, has been reduced by the full amount of the check, leaving you with only $6.19 in the bank. A call to your boss doesn't help, as all he says is that he "had to pay my suppliers first. I'll get you the money by next payday."

However, two weeks later, you are only paid the amount you are due for working the immediately preceding two weeks. Nothing is said about the paycheck which bounced. Fortunately, you are able to quit your job at the donut shop and get on at a gourmet bagel establishment. But you're still stuck with a month-old rubber paycheck.

You can sue in Small Claims Court to recover the amount you are due when a paycheck bounces, or even when no check was tendered by your employer. Colorado law states that if you are laid off or terminated, you are entitled to be paid immediately. If you quit, your check is due on your next regular payday.

If there is a legitimate dispute concerning the amount of money an employee is due, state law still requires the employer to pay the employee the full amount of wages which are undisputed. The law says that the acceptance of the undisputed amount by the employee does not mean that the employee is waiving claim to the rest of the money due the employee. Don't let an employer try to pull that one on you.

Remember to bring suit against the proper defendant. The defendant may be the owner of a business if it is a sole proprietorship, or all partners and the partnership itself if the business is a partnership, or a corporation. If you are unsure of the structure of the employer's business, call the Secretary of State or your local sales tax licensing office. You may also be able to get this information from your paycheck stub.

As described in chapter two, you can bring an action in the amount of the wages due plus a penalty equal to either 50 percent of the amount of wages due or the amount of wages payable to you for ten working days, whichever is greater. To seek this penalty, you must first make a written demand for payment to the employer within 60 days of the date the wages were due you.

Your returned paycheck is your best evidence that you are still owed money for unpaid wages. Time sheets can also prove that you worked during a given period of time. Other employees who can attest to your having worked the hours in question can be beneficial to your case. You can prove your hourly wage or monthly salary by using your most recent paycheck stub to show your rate of pay.

The law says that an employer can't harass, threaten or fire an employee who files an action to recover unpaid wages for actual hours worked. Doing so makes the employer vulnerable to criminal penalties.

You can also seek assistance from the Colorado Department of Labor. Call (303) 572-2241 if you would like to file a claim with that office against your employer for unpaid wages.

SUING A CONTRACTOR

Homeowners and small business owners sometimes find it necessary to sue contractors who have not adequately performed or completed jobs such as remodeling or landscaping. These cases may be brought in Small Claims Court.

Be sure you can show that your agreement with the contractor, either written or verbal, specified the work that was to be done. Take pictures of the work that was done, if any. A key component of a case like this is an expert witness who can testify that the work done was inadequate, incomplete, or not up to the common standards for the type of work involved. A witness like this is especially critical if the contractor lines up an expert witness to say that the work done by the contractor was, in fact, above industry standards.

If you were fortunate enough to have hired a bonded contractor, you may be able to bring in the bonding company— also known as the "surety"—into the case as another defendant. Doing this can prove essential if the contractor is someone who has gone out of business or left town before you filed suit. Be sure the bonding company is served with the complaint, too.

MOTOR VEHICLE REPAIR CASES

Chapter two briefly discusses how you can sue for triple damages in cases in which a customer of a motor vehicle repair garage was not given a written or verbal estimate prior to the commencement of work on the vehicle. If your claim is based on the lack of an estimate, follow these procedures exactly before you seek triple damages. You must remember that your first step is to demand a refund, in writing, from the garage before filing suit. This demand must precede the action by at least ten days, not counting Saturdays, Sundays, or holidays.

Other motor vehicle repair cases may deal with repairs which have not taken care of the problem which originally caused you to seek the services of the garage, even if the price for the repairs was the same as that provided in the estimate. What if you took your car to a mechanic, paid $600 to have an oil leak fixed, and got home only to realize the car still leaks oil from the same spot?

There are several strategies which can help you prevail in cases such as this. Some involve merely being a smart consumer.

Colorado law allows you to get your original parts back from the repair shop, as long as you make this request before the repairs begin. Having the original part in your possession may prove helpful, depending on the nature of the repairs.

Your next step is to have your car examined by another mechanic. Explain the problem, and what was supposedly done by the other garage to fix it. You may or may not have to pay for this service. Get a written report of the mechanics findings.

Next, give the first garage the results of the opinion you have gotten from the other mechanic. It's possible that the first garage will look at your car again, and even fix it for free. You won't know if you don't ask.

If the garage doesn't go along, draft and send a demand letter as outlined in chapter three. If this results in no response, file a case in Small Claims Court, and prepare for the trial.

Remember that you may need to become better acquainted with the subject of auto mechanics. An expert witness is very important in these types of cases. Perhaps the second mechanic who checked your car would be willing to help you in this way. Keep in mind that you'll be up against the garage's mechanics, who are probably more familiar with the the topic, in general, and what was done to your car, in particular, than you are.

Cases such as these are often won based on the effectiveness of the court presentation. Be especially thorough in gathering your evidence, including all documents relating to the case, as well as in preparing your witnesses. If you can explain your case in plain English to the court, you greatly increase your chances of winning. Don't go in to a case like this thinking that it will be enough to say that your car went into the shop broken and still wasn't fixed when it came out. A well prepared case is essential.

MOTOR VEHICLE ACCIDENT CASES

In a case involving a motor vehicle accident, be sure to sue both the driver of the vehicle and the owner of the vehicle, if they are different. Note that a business or corporation may be the owner of the vehicle. You must serve each defendant with a copy of the *Notice, Claim and Summons to Appear.* Also keep this information for later use in the collection process.

Find out if anyone witnessed the accident. An eyewitness who supports your position can provide invaluable information, both to you and the judge. If there was a formal police report filed, a witness may be listed there. The police report may contain other information which backs up your case.

Accident cases are among those which can benefit greatly from diagrams. Follow the tips found in chapter six. Remember, it will not be held against you or your case if you are the one who prepares the diagram, as long as it is an accurate depiction of the accident. Be neat, and pay attention to detail.

Photographs of the accident scene and the damage done can be helpful in setting the stage for your argument. In some instances, photographs can even help prove your case by showing, for example, that only a car moving eastbound could have caused the damage to the driver's side of a westbound car.

Prove your damages through the presentation of estimates for the repairs. Getting more than one estimate is prudent. If the work has already been completed, use the receipt as proof of your repair costs.

SUITS AGAINST GOVERNMENT AGENCIES AND EMPLOYEES

In general, you are allowed to bring actions against state and local governmental entities in Small Claims Court. These agencies can include the State of Colorado, counties, cities, and special districts.

Typically, your first step in the process is the filing of a claim with the governmental unit in question. If your car is struck by a garbage truck from the City of Aurora, go first to the Aurora City Hall and complete a claim form. This form will be reviewed by the City Attorney and the City Council. If they agree to reimburse you, an action in Small Claims Court is unnecessary. If your claim is denied, you may then file a case. If you are not sure who to serve, call the office where you filed your claim and ask who is the proper individual or office to serve with a lawsuit. Be sure to bring to the hearing any paperwork you received from the governmental office which denied your claim.

Suits against the federal government may not be brought in Small Claims Court. However, you may garnish employees of federal agencies, including the post office. Again, call the relevant agency to determine where best to serve a writ of garnishment.

Chapter 8: Enforcement of Restrictive Covenants on Residential Property

A SPECIAL CATEGORY OF CASES

The rules and procedures of Small Claims Court discussed in this book apply to all kinds of cases, including those involving car accidents, product refunds, landlord-tenant disputes, bad check debt and contracts. All types of cases use the same forms, and are dealt with in much the same manner for purposes of enforcing judgments. There is, however, one exception to this one-size-fits-all rule in Small Claims Court.

Cases involving actions to enforce the provisions of restrictive covenants on residential property have their own special procedures in Small Claims Court. They also use an entirely separate set of forms. While most of the usual Small Claims Court procedures used in the typical case are in force, there are several twists in restrictive covenant cases.

These cases involve proceedings designed to ensure compliance by homeowners with the covenants which bind them and their neighbors. These covenants can cover a wide range of topics, from the color houses are painted, to television antennas, to the storage of recreational vehicles on homeowners' property. The exact language and extent of the coverage differs from housing development to housing development. Almost all new housing developments are governed by a set of restrictive covenants, which bind the buyers of new homes as well as anyone who purchases a previously occupied house in that development. An estimated one in ten people in the United States now lives in a community with covenants.

The plaintiffs in these cases can be either individual homeowners or the homeowner's association charged with enforcing the covenants. The defendant is the owner of the home which is the subject of the alleged violation, as well as any current resident occupants of the home if it is being rented by another party. The plaintiff alleges that the defendant home-owner is out of compliance with some term of the covenants, and asks the court to order the defendant to meet the requirements of the covenants.

It is a requirement that a defendant homeowner be subject to a set of restrictive covenants which apply to the residential property in question. Cases may not be brought by a homeowner against another if no covenants govern their neighborhood. Older developments may not have such a set of covenants in place.

You can usually find a copy of your restrictive covenants in the papers you completed when you purchased your home. They can also be found at the office of the County Clerk and Recorder.

INITIATING THE ACTION

The case is begun by the filing of a complaint,using the same *Notice, Claim and Summons to Appear for Trial* form as used in all other small claims cases. It is completed in much the same manner. The section where the plaintiff states his claim requires more detailed information than the standard Small Claims Court case. The plaintiff must list the address of the defendant's property, how the defendant is violating the covenants, and how much it will cost to remedy the violation. This amount must be less than the small claims limit of $7,500. The plaintiff must state why he has a right to enforce the covenant, and what he wants the court to order the defendant to do.

The usual small claims rules regarding venue apply in these cases, except that the case may also be filed in the county where the real property in question is located. The rules of service of process described in Chapter 4 also apply. The same fee schedule applies, based on the amount needed to address the covenant violation. The Small Claims Court laws and rules pertaining to restrictive covenants can be found in Appendix D at the end of this book.

The case must focus solely on the defendant's breach of the restrictive covenants. A case may not be brought in Small Claims Court to enforce a restrictive covenant if it affects the title to the property.

Spouses who are both listed as owners of the home on the deed may be sued using a single complaint. However, separate complaints must be served on other owners, as well as on the current resident if that person is not the owner of the property.

TEMPORARY ORDERS

A feature of restrictive covenant cases not found in any other action in Small Claims Court is the ability of the plaintiff to ask the court for a temporary order directing the defendant to comply immediately with the restrictive covenant before the defendant has had an opportunity to be heard in court. To do this, the plaintiff must attach to the complaint a certified copy of the deed to the defendant's property and a certified copy of the restrictive covenants. Copies of these items must also be served on the defendant. For more information on how to serve these documents, see Service of Process in Chapter 4.

The hearing regarding the temporary order will be scheduled for the earliest time the court is available. It is held "ex parte," meaning that the defendant is not present at the hearing. The plaintiff must prove to the court that there is a "substantial likelihood" that the plaintiff will prevail at a trial on the merits of the claim and that the plaintiff will suffer "irreparable damage" if a temporary order is not issued. The plaintiff can do this via whatever evidence is necessary. If the court is satisfied, it will then issue a temporary order as well as a citation to the defendant ordering him to appear in court at the stated date and time to show why the temporary order should not be made permanent. The defendant is then served with a copy of the *Temporary Order and Citation* form which is available at the court. Temporary orders are not appealable.

Small Claims Court, _____ County, Colorado

Court Address:

PLAINTIFF(S): _____

Address: _____

City/State/Zip: _____

Phone: Home _____ Work _____

v.

DEFENDANT(S): _____

Address: _____

City/State/Zip: _____

Phone: Home _____ Work: _____

▲   **COURT USE ONLY**   ▲

Case Number:

Division: Courtroom:

TEMPORARY ORDER AND CITATION
ENFORCEMENT OF RESTRICTIVE COVENANT ON RESIDENTIAL PROPERTY

THIS MATTER is heard ex parte. _____ appears on behalf of the Plaintiff(s). The Court has examined the claim filed, and has heard the testimony of the Plaintiff(s), and:

THE COURT FINDS:

1.   The Small Claims Court appears to have subject matter jurisdiction over this action.
2.   The Plaintiff(s) is/are a proper party in interest.
3.   Defendant(s) owns/possesses the residential property identified in the claim.
4.   There is a restrictive covenant of record, which restricts the use of the property.
5.   It appears that the Defendant(s) is/are in violation of such covenant by: _____
     _____
     _____

     It appears that there is a substantial likelihood Plaintiff(s) will prevail at trial on the merits of this case.

6.   It appears that irreparable harm will accrue to the Plaintiff(s) unless a temporary order issues immediately, relating to initiating or continuing any violation of the covenant.

IT IS THEREFORE ORDERED that immediately upon service of a copy of this TEMPORARY ORDER AND CITATION, the Defendant(s) shall: _____
_____
_____

IT IS FURTHER ORDERED THAT THE DEFENDANT(S) IS/ARE CITED AND ORDERED TO APPEAR
before this Court at the address stated above in the caption in Courtroom/Division _____
on (date) _____, at (time) _____, to show cause, if any, why this TEMPORARY ORDER should not be made permanent. If the Defendant(s) fails to appear in Court on the above date and time, the TEMPORARY ORDER shall be made permanent, if the Plaintiff(s) request(s), and a bench warrant may issue for the Defendant's arrest. A private process server may serve this order.

ANY VIOLATION OF THIS TEMPORARY ORDER MAY CONSTITUTE CONTEMPT OF COURT, WHICH MAY BE PUNISHED BY CONTEMPT, FINES, DAMAGES, ATTORNEY FEES, AND COSTS.

BY THE COURT

Date: _____

_____
□ Judge □ Magistrate

JDF 258 R9/01 TEMPORARY ORDER AND CITATION ENFORCEMENT OF RESTRICTIVE COVENANT ON
RESIDENTIAL PROPERTY (Page 1 of 2)

PERMANENT ORDERS

After a temporary order has been issued, the plaintiff and defendant must appear at the hearing to determine whether the temporary order becomes permanent. A similar hearing will be held if the plaintiff did not seek a temporary order, but merely scheduled a hearing at the time the complaint was filed, as in any other type of small claims case. This hearing will look much like the standard small claims trial, with the plaintiff first arguing how the defendant has violated the covenants and why he should be forced to comply with them. The plaintiff can offer evidence, including witnesses, to prove his case. The defendant is then given an opportunity to present his case along with any supporting evidence. The plaintiff will still have to prove his case if the defendant does not appear at the hearing.

The court then either accepts or rejects the plaintiff's claim. If the court rules in favor of the plaintiff, it will issue a permanent order directing the defendant to comply with the restrictive covenants governing his property. The court will specify exactly how the defendant must comply by issuing a form called JDF 260, *Permanent Order.*

The defendant must take action to comply with the order, or file an appeal to the District Court, following the usual Small Claims Court rules. Violation of the order by the defendant may constitute contempt of court. The defendant may be issued a citation requiring that he appear before a county judge to explain why the order has not yet been complied with. If the defendant fails to appear for such a hearing, the court may issue a warrant for the defendant's arrest. The defendant can also be fined, imprisoned, and assessed attorney's fees and costs.

Small Claims Court, _____ County, Colorado Court Address: **PLAINTIFF(S):** _____ Address: _____ City/State/Zip: _____ Phone: Home _____ Work _____ v. **DEFENDANT(S):** _____ Address: _____ City/State/Zip: _____ Phone: Home _____ Work _____	 ▲ **COURT USE ONLY** ▲ Case Number: Division: Courtroom:

PERMANENT ORDER

The Court has jurisdiction over the persons and subject matter of this action. Venue is proper before the Court.

☐ Plaintiff(s) is/are ordered to deliver on or before (date) _____, the following property

_____
_____
_____

☐ Defendant(s) is/are ordered to deliver on or before (date) _____, the following property

_____
_____
_____

☐ Plaintiff(s) ☐ Defendant(s) own(s)/possess(es) residential property properly identified and addressed as

_____

There is a restrictive covenant of record that restricts the use of the residential property.
☐ Plaintiff(s) ☐ Defendant(s) has/have violated the provisions of the covenant and is/are ordered to comply
as follows: _____

_____

on or before (date) _____.

**VIOLATION OF THIS ORDER MAY CONSTITUTE CONTEMPT OF COURT. JUDGMENT FOR
ADDITIONAL DAMAGES MAY BE ENTERED AGAINST YOU.**

BY THE COURT

Date: _____

         _____
         ☐ Judge ☐ Magistrate

CERTIFICATE OF MAILING

I hereby certify that on (date) _____, I mailed a true and correct copy of the PERMANENT
ORDER, by placing it in the United States Mail, postage pre-paid to the parties at the addresses listed above.

Date: _____

         _____
         Clerk of Court/ Deputy

JDF 260 9/01 PERMANENT ORDER

POINTERS FOR PLAINTIFFS AND DEFENDANTS

While small claims cases involving restrictive covenants on residential property have many of their own unique rules and procedures, the underlying philosophy is the same. The case is being heard in Small Claims Court to allow each party to present his or her case in a forum where attorneys are not allowed and the legal rules are relaxed. In this way, the dispute can be resolved with a minimum of cost and inconvenience to the parties.

Plaintiffs should begin their case by sending the defendant a demand letter prior to initiating a court action. The plaintiff should also get at least three estimates of the cost of remedying the covenant violation. After filing and service of the complaint, the plaintiff should prepare a case outline and gather all relevant information, evidence, and witnesses required to successfully prove the case. Adequate preparation is just as important in property covenant cases as it is in other small claims actions.

In response to the original complaint, the defendant may do nothing, file a response, or file a counterclaim. The usual rules regarding timing and fees apply here. The defendant may also seek to have the case transferred to the County Court, either because he wants to be represented by an attorney or because the amount of his counterclaim exceeds the Small Claims Court dollar limit. If the defendant does not appear in court for the hearing, a default judgment can be entered against him.

A plaintiff who prevails in one of these cases may not enforce his claim via a writ of garnishment or other remedy described in Chapter 11. This is because the defendant really does not owe the plaintiff money, but rather he owes the plaintiff compliance with the same restrictive covenants which bind the plaintiff. The remedy, then, is the permanent order issued by the court directing the defendant to comply with the covenants.

Chapter 9: The Trial

OBSERVING

If you are unfamiliar with the court process and have never before participated in a small claims case, you probably do not know what to expect from the actual trial. Do not rely on what you have seen on television, either in fictionalized programs or on broadcasts from famous cases in the news. You should not plan to use courtroom theatrics to win your case, nor will you be expected to present detailed evidence of the results of tests performed on DNA samples.

The best way to learn how small claims cases are handled in court is to observe some actual cases for yourself. Hearings are open to the public, and you are free to drop in and learn. Call the court in advance to see if any hearings are scheduled for a time when you are free. You can get valuable pointers from other small claims parties, and you may even chance upon a case with facts similar to those in your case. This type of observation also provides you with the chance to become comfortable with the the the atmosphere and layout of the courtroom, and to see how the parties, witnesses, and the judge interact. You may get some clue as to what judges like and do not like. Observing small claims hearings also gives you the advantage of knowing that when your case comes up, it won't be the first time you have seen a small claims case.

PRACTICE, PRACTICE, PRACTICE

Take your case outline and merge it with what you have learned about small claims hearings based on your observations to come up with an effective presentation of your case. Focus on the relevant facts in an orderly manner. Practice your case presentation by yourself until you feel comfortable. Then practice it in front of family, friends, or co-workers at lunch. Remember, the facts of your case may be obvious to you, but they are not to someone who has not been through what you have. Your presentation is your chance to make the facts of your case clear to the judge who will rule on your claim.

This type of preparation will not only make you more comfortable at the hearing, but also will increase the likelihood of your prevailing in the case.

DETAILS, DETAILS

Be sure to take care of all practical matters ahead of time so that you can focus on your presentation on the trial date. Make absolutely sure you know where the courtroom is. Know how long it will take you to get to the courthouse, and where you can park. Have all necessary copies made, and make sure arrangements for your witnesses are in place.

Pay special attention to the materials you will bring to court to prove your case. Note those items which you plan to present to the judge in support of your position. Separate these from your notes and your case outline so you do not get them mixed up at the trial. Determine in what order these materials should be presented, based on your case outline. Have the Certificate of Personal Service ready, too.

Think about what you will wear to court. There is no need for men to wear a suit and tie or for women to wear a dress to the hearing. Remember, this is a court of law and it is best to dress respectfully. Avoid wearing ratty, torn clothing or t-shirts with questionable messages on them. This will only distract the court from your case presentation. You need not dress up, but it is best not to dress down, either. Just be yourself.

SHOWTIME!

After all the anxiety you have probably built up in preparation for the court hearing, it is disappointing to know that the first thing you will have to do in the courtroom is wait. Your case may be scheduled for 10 a.m., but probably so are several others. Your case may not be heard until 10:30 or 11:00. Be sure your witnesses have allowed ample time for this type of delay.

The trial is meant to be a simple, informal hearing where you present your case to the judge and the defendant does likewise. It is normal to be somewhat intimidated by the trappings of an unfamiliar court process. However, do not let this intimidation draw you away from your focus on your case presentation.

The moment will arrive when your case is called by the judge or clerk. You will approach the bench, possibly at the same time as other parties in other cases. Your witnesses should stay seated in the audience.

At this time, the judge may launch into a lecture about the role of the Small Claims Court and what you can expect from it, as well as how she intends to proceed. She may also raise the possibility of settlement with the other party, even at this late date. The rules of Small Claims Court specifically state that the court may require settlement discussions between the parties prior to the trial. Some judges push this option very hard. They will do everything short of ordering you to talk about the case with the other party. You may be asked if you are open to such discussions. Answer honestly. You always retain the right to have the trial even if you agree to participate in a settlement discussion. The rationale behind this push to settle is that parties are more satisfied with agreements they had a part in shaping as opposed to rulings issued from on high by a judge.

If you do go into a settlement discussion with the other party, you will be shown to a conference room to hold the talks. Consider the possibility that the defendant may be willing to bargain in good faith. Avoid the idea that you owe it to yourself to follow through with the trial because, after all, you put so much time and effort into your presentation. What you really owe yourself is an openness to the possibility that you could reach a reasonable settlement with the defendant. But remember, no matter how much the judge wants you to settle, you are under no obligation to do so.

If you do reach a settlement with the defendant during these discussions, go back into the courtroom and wait for the judge to call your case again. You can then explain the settlement agreement to the judge. You will then be asked if you are satisfied with the terms of the agreement. If you both agree, you will be asked if you wish the case to be dismissed "with prejudice" or "without prejudice." A case dismissed with prejudice cannot ever be filed again in any court by either party. A dismissal without prejudice leaves open the possibility of either party raising a legal action based on this case sometime in the future.

(handwritten margin note: if settled out of court, be sure till the judge you want to)

PRESENTING YOUR CASE

If no settlement is reached, or if no such discussions are held, it is time to present your case to the judge. She will ask you to approach the table or podium. Be sure to go to the appropriate location for the plaintiff or defendant. You will then be asked to state your name and to spell your last name for the record. Be sure to speak clearly into the microphone. Your words are being tape recorded to create a record of the hearing.

The judge will then ask you why you are suing the defendant. State your basic position now, but do not respond with a lengthy speech detailing your whole case yet. The better approach is to respond to questions from the judge which allow you to make the important points from your case.

Whatever you do, **do not argue** with the judge. Also do not roll your eyes or glare in response to something the judge has said. Remember, you want the judge to be on your side.

(handwritten margin note: If witnesses!)

You are free to call your witnesses at the appropriate point during the presentation of your case. The witness will be called forward and asked to state his name for the record before providing testimony. You can also offer your pieces of evidence by presenting them to the judge for inspection.

(handwritten margin note: Questions can be asked to defendant)

During the presentation of your case, you may ask the defendant questions. The defendant can, in turn, pose questions to you and your witnesses.

Remember to stick to the facts of your case. Do not state conclusions. The judge's job is to reach conclusions. Yours is to ensure that the facts presented allow the judge to reach the conclusion you desire.

After you have completed your presentation, the judge will ask the defendant to respond. The defendant may then make a presentation of his position, including the offering of evidence and the calling of witnesses. Do not interrupt or argue during the other presentation.

When both sides are finished, the judge will probably ask each party a few more questions to clearly understand the case. Some of these questions may call for information you have already stated, but give the answer cheerfully anyway.

You are now at the big moment. The judge will issue a ruling, including an explanation of how she arrived at her decision. This ruling could be for everything you asked for in your claim, or for a portion of it. Of course, the judge may rule in favor of the defendant, and may award you nothing, and could even make an award for the defendant based on his counterclaim. Accept this ruling without any attempt to sway the judge one last time.

SAM'S CASE

Sam arrived at court with George in tow at 9:45 a.m. In the courtroom were about twelve other people, two of whom were in the front of the room speaking with the magistrate. Sam and George sat down.

Bob walked in at about ten minutes after ten, while another case was in progress. He sat down on the opposite side of the room from Sam and George.

At 10:20, the magistrate called the cases set for 10:00 a.m. Three cases were called, and all the plaintiffs and defendants approached the front of the room and formed a line parallel to the magistrate's bench. The magistrate told the parties how the cases would proceed, and urged them to consider one last try at settling the case. The magistrate then asked each plaintiff and defendant individually if they would agree to meet with the other party outside of the courtroom. Both the parties in each of the cases ahead of Sam's agreed to talk about a settlement, and they left the courtroom.

The magistrate next turned to Sam, asking him if he would consider meeting with Bob to discuss a settlement. Because he had put a lot of effort into his case so far, and because he felt he was on the right side of the case, Sam was eager to present his case to the court. However, he saw no harm in a chat with Bob, and told the magistrate that, yes, he would talk to Bob.

Bob, however, would have none of it. He told the magistrate

that he had nothing to say to Sam, and that he wanted to get right down to the trial. The magistrate, with his other cases in settlement conferences, decided to start the trial immediately.

Sam and Bob took their respective places by the podiums marked "plaintiff" and "defendant." The magistrate called the case number, and asked each party to state his name and the spelling of his last name for the record directly into the microphone. He then asked Sam what this case was about.

Sam said he was seeking $1,000 from Mr. Lee in compensation for trees Sam had planted on Bob's property. He said Mr. Lee had paid him the first half of the agreed upon price, but that he now refused to pay the rest. Sam did not elaborate any further.

The magistrate told Sam to proceed. Sam gave a copy of his demand letter to the magistrate and to Bob, as well as a copy of the invoice he had given to Bob when the trees were planted. Sam then went on to describe in detail how the deal between he and Bob came about, and how he had planted the trees in Bob's back-yard. He then told the magistrate how he had contacted Bob about payment of the remaining $1,000, and how Bob had replied that he could not pay. Sam then stated that he had sent the demand letter to Bob before filing suit in Small Claims Court.

Sam next turned to the photographs. He gave them to the magistrate, who then invited Bob forward to view them. Sam told how he had taken these photos ten days before, and pointed out that the trees appeared to be healthy. The magistrate entered the photos as exhibits for the plaintiff.

Sam then called upon George. George stated his name for the record and told the magistrate that he had been in the nursery business for seventeen years and was very familiar with Colorado Blue Spruce trees. He told the court how he had helped Sam choose the trees that morning, and that they were in perfect condition at that time, and that he saw nothing to indicate that they were unhealthy in any way. The magistrate asked George if he recognized the trees in Sam's photos. George took another look at the pictures and replied that, yes, the trees in the photos looked like the ones Sam had purchased from his nursery that day in May.

Sam closed by saying that there was a deal between he and Bob, that Sam had delivered as promised on their deal, and that Bob had then refused to go along with his part of the bargain. Sam ended by asking the court to award him the full $1,000 he was seeking, plus costs.

The magistrate paused for a moment to review Sam's evidence. He then turned to Bob and asked him to tell the court why what Mr. Grant had said was not correct. He also noted that Bob had counterclaimed for the $1,000 he had already paid Sam.

Bob said that he agreed with Sam that there was a deal concerning the trees between he and Sam. He said he had paid Sam $1,000 in good faith before the trees were delivered and planted. He continued by saying that he had come home from work on May 24 to find the trees in his backyard and an invoice from Sam in his mailbox. He was preparing, he said, to pay the balance of the bill to Sam several days later when he noticed the trees looked extremely dry and were changing color from green to brown at the ends of many branches. He held off paying Sam, and watched the trees get worse over the next two weeks. He told the magistrate that he decided then that he would not pay Sam any more money for trees that were dying. He also wanted the court to order Sam to return his first $1,000 payment, and order Sam to pay Bob's filing fees.

While Sam struggled to hold his tongue, the magistrate asked Bob if he had any proof of the condition of the trees. Bob replied that he did not have anything with him, and that he should have taken some pictures of the trees himself, because, he said, "you should see them, your honor. They look really bad." The magistrate replied by asking Bob if Sam's pictures were from Bob's house. Bob said that those were his trees in the photographs, but that the photos did not really show the actual condition of the trees.

The magistrate then asked Bob if he had received Sam's demand letter. Bob said he had. The magistrate also asked Bob if he had told Sam that he was suffering financial difficulties and, as a result, could not pay Sam. Bob admitted having a conversation with Sam, but he said it was the state of the trees, not his money problems, which kept him from paying Sam. "I have the money," Bob told the judge.

The magistrate asked Sam and Bob if either of them had any more to say. They both answered no. The magistrate then said he would take a moment to consider the case before issuing a ruling.

Sam stared at his shoes while the magistrate flipped through the papers and looked again at the photographs. About thirty seconds later, the magistrate announced that he was finding in favor of the plaintiff, Sam Grant, against the defendant, Robert Lee, and that he was denying the defendant's counterclaim. He was entering judgment against the defendant for $1,000, plus $38.80 in service fees and $23 in filing fees, for a total judgment of $1,061.80. The magistrate explained that the plaintiff had fully presented the case for his claim and had backed it up with appropriate evidence. The defendant, he said, had only made assertions with nothing to support them. Based on the evidence presented, said the magistrate, he had no choice but to find for the plaintiff.

Sam tried unsuccessfully to suppress a big grin.

DEFAULT CASES

What if the defendant in your case does not show up for the hearing? This can happen when the defendant has never responded to your original complaint and also when the defendant has filed a response, even a counterclaim.

If your case is called in the courtroom and the defendant is not present, make sure you answer the judge's call. She will call again for the defendant. If there is no answer, you will immediately be asked if proper service was made on the defendant. You must then produce the Certificate of Personal Service on the green copy of the complaint, or direct the judge to the return receipt card in the court file. The court wants to be very sure that the defendant was actually served with the paperwork before it issues a ruling in his absence. If the judge is convinced that there was proper service, you can ask that a default judgment be entered against the defendant. You will still have to explain your case to the judge. Be sure to state what happened, why the defendant owes you, and how you calculated the amount of your claim. If you can do this, it is likely that the court will grant you the default judgment.

If a defendant appears at the hearing but the plaintiff does not, the claim against the defendant will probably be dismissed without prejudice. This means the plaintiff may never pursue the claim against the defendant.

Congratulations! If all went well, you now have a judgment in your favor against the defendant. However, even though the trial is over, your case may not be.

Chapter 10: After the Trial

THE COLLECTION PROCESS BEGINS

After you have obtained a judgment against the defendant, your legal relationship with the defendant has changed. You are now the judgment creditor, and the defendant is now the judgment debtor. The law grants certain rights to creditors in their efforts to collect from their debtors.

As soon as the judge in your case grants you a judgment against the defendant, you may begin the process which can lead to a collection of the amount of your claim. If the defendant is present, the judge can ask that the defendant pay the amount to you right then and there. She may ask the defendant if he can write you a check immediately. Some will actually do this because they want to be done with the matter. Many, however, will have conveniently forgotten their checkbooks. If this is the case, ask the judge to order the debtor to answer interrogatories.

"Interrogatories" is a legal term for questions. The court has two standard interrogatory forms, JDF 252A and JDF 252B. The first is the short form and consists of six questions that are designed to be answered by the defendant in the courtroom before he or she leaves.

The second form is the long form and asks many more questions in more detail. Don't count on your defendant knowing the answer to everyone of these questions right then and there. These forms are available in the clerk's office. The court can order the defendant to go immediately to the clerk's office, get a form, and answer the questions it contains. The questions seek financial information from the debtor, and are intended to help you collect your money. The questions inquire about such things as the debtor's employment or business, home rental or ownership status, income, and bank accounts. They also ask about cars and real estate the debtor may own.

If possible, remain at the court while the defendant answers the interrogatories. You can ask the judge to order the defendant to answer any questions that were skipped. This information can prove invaluable when you go about collecting your judgment.

You can get these questions answered even if the defendant did not show up for the court hearing. Ask the court to issue the interrogatories to the defendant. The court will complete the top section of the motion, tell the defendant when to appear in court to answer the questions, and mail the form to him. The defendant may be sent these wherever he is known to be, even in jail. The interrogatories can also be served personally on the defendant.

Use of the interrogatories is not mandatory, and they may be requested after the actual trial date. It is just that the defendant may prove to be elusive later on—and you will benefit if you can acquire this information about the debtor now.

Small Claims Court, _____ County, Colorado
Court Address:

PLAINTIFF(S): _____

Address: _____

City/State/Zip: _____

Phone: Home _____ Work _____

v.

DEFENDANT(S): _____

Address: _____

City/State/Zip: _____

Phone: Home _____ Work _____

▲ COURT USE ONLY ▲

Case Number:

Division: Courtroom:

MOTION AND ORDER FOR INTERROGATORIES – SHORT FORM

MOTION

Judgment was entered on: (date) _____, against the:
☐ Plaintiff ☐ Defendant   By: ☐ Default ☐ After trial
The judgment remains unsatisfied. Pursuant to Rule 518(a), C.R.C.P., the ☐ judgment creditor requests or the ☐ Court finds that the judgment debtor should be required to answer the following interrogatories.

ORDER

☐ Pursuant to Rule 518(a), at the request of the judgment creditor. **OR**

On the Court's review of the above Motion **IT IS ORDERED:**

☐ That the judgment debtor shall answer the following questions and file the answers with the Court ☐ immediately ☐ within ten days after service of these interrogatories upon the judgment debtor, or in lieu thereof, pay the judgment in full. **OR**

☐ That the judgment debtor answer the questions and appear in Court at (date) _____ at (time) _____.

FAILURE TO TRUTHFULLY AND COMPLETELY ANSWER ALL OF THESE QUESTIONS AND RETURN THEM WITHIN TEN DAYS TO THE CLERK OF THE COURT, SMALL CLAIMS COURT, SHALL CAUSE A CITATION TO BE ISSUED FOR CONTEMPT OF COURT. A FINDING OF CONTEMPT BY THE COURT MAY RESULT IN A FINE OR JAIL SENTENCE.

Date: _____

_____
☐ Judge ☐ Magistrate

INTERROGATORIES

1. What is your full legal name: _____
   List any other names you have been known by: _____
   Home address: _____
   Home phone number: _____ Work phone number: _____
   Date of birth: _____ Social Security Number: _____
   Drivers license number: _____ State: _____

2. As to your employment, complete the following:
   The employer's/company's name: _____
   Address of employer: _____
   Phone number: _____ Supervisor's name: _____
   You are paid: ☐ hourly $ _____ ☐ monthly $ _____ ☐ or your annual rate of pay you
   earn $ _____ ☐ you are paid commissions, the manner in which commissions are calculated are:
   _____

The days or days of the month on which you are paid: _____

3. As to your bank accounts, complete the following: List the name and address and account number of every bank, savings and loan, credit union or other financial institution holding any funds that you have deposited or that you are allowed to withdraw without obtaining another person's signature.

Name of Bank Savings & Loan/Credit Union	Address/Location City/State	Account Number
Name of Bank Savings & Loan/Credit Union	Address/Location City/State	Account Number
Name of Bank Savings & Loan/Credit Union	Address/Location City/State	Account Number
Name of Bank Savings & Loan/Credit Union	Address/Location City/State	Account Number
Name of Bank Savings & Loan/Credit Union	Address/Location City/State	Account Number

4. State the full and correct address of all real estate you own or have an interest in:

Address	City/County State
Address	City/County State
Address	City/County State
Address	City/County State

5. As to debts owed to you, complete the following. List the name and address of every person who owes you money and the amount owed to you:

Name	Address City/State	$ _____ Amount owed
Name	Address City/State	$ _____ Amount owed
Name	Address City/State	$ _____ Amount owed
Name	Address City/State	$ _____ Amount owed

6. As to insurance coverage, complete the following: List the name and address of any insurance company providing liability coverage, including policy numbers with agent's name.

Name of Insurance Company – Name of Agent	Address/Location City/State	Policy Number
Name of Insurance Company – Name of Agent	Address/Location City/State	Policy Number
Name of Insurance Company – Name of Agent	Address/Location City/State	Policy Number

UNDER PENALTIES OF PERJURY, I DECLARE THAT THESE STATEMENTS ARE TRUE AND CORRECT.

Date: _____   _____
                                                Judgment debtor's signature

Subscribed and affirmed, or sworn to before me in the County of _____, State of _____, this _____ day of _____, 20 _____.

My commission expires: _____   _____
                                                         Notary Public/Clerk of Court/Deputy Clerk

JDF 252A 9/01 MOTION AND ORDER FOR INTERROGATORIES – SHORT FORM (Page 2 of 3)

Case Name _____ v. _____ Case Number: _____

AFFIDAVIT OF SERVICE
(Must be returned to Court)

I served a copy of the foregoing Interrogatories, on the following:

Name   **Date**   **Place**

If the person on whom service was made is not the named party to be served, I served the Interrogatories:

☐   At the regular place of abode of the person to be served, by leaving the Notice with a person over the age of18 years who regularly resides at the place of abode. (Identify relationship to defendant _____.)

☐   At the regular place of business of the person to be served, by leaving the Notice with that person's secretary, bookkeeper, chief clerk, office receptionist/assistant or partner. (Circle title of person who was served.)

☐   By leaving the Notice with a partner, limited partner, associate, manager, elected official, receptionist/assistant, bookkeeper or general agent of the partnership, limited liability company, or other non-corporate entity, which was to be served. (Circle title of person who was served.)

☐   By leaving the Notice with an officer, manager, receptionist/assistant, legal assistant, paid legal advisor or general agent, registered agent for service of process, stockholder or principal employee of the corporation that was to be served. (Circle title of person who was served.)

I am over the age of 18 years, and I am not an interested party in this matter.

I have charged the following fees for my services in this matter:

☐ Private process server
☐ Sheriff, _____ County
     Fee $ _____ Mileage $ _____

_____
Signature of Process Server

_____
Name (Print or type)

Subscribed and affirmed, or sworn to before me in the County of _____, State of _____, this _____ day of _____, 20 _____.

My commission expires: _____

_____
Notary Public

CERTIFICATE OF SERVICE BY MAILING
(To be performed by Clerk within three days of filing)

I hereby certify that on (date) _____, I mailed a true and correct copy of the MOTION AND ORDER FOR INTERROGATORIES – SHORT FORM, by placing it in the United States Mail, postage pre-paid to the Defendant(s) at the address(es) listed above.

By: _____
                 Clerk of Court/Deputy Clerk

☐ (If applicable) Plaintiff(s) notified of non-service on (date) _____. Clerk's Initials _____

JDF 252A 9/01 MOTION AND ORDER FOR INTERROGATORIES – SHORT FORM (Page 3 of 3)

Small Claims Court, _____ County, Colorado
Court Address:

PLAINTIFF(S): _____

Address: _____

City/State/Zip: _____

Phone: Home _____ Work _____

v.

DEFENDANT(S): _____

Address: _____

City/State/Zip: _____

Phone: Home _____ Work _____

▲ COURT USE ONLY ▲

Case Number:

Division: Courtroom:

MOTION AND ORDER FOR INTERROGATORIES – LONG FORM

The judgment creditor, _____, requests this Court to issue an order requiring the judgment debtor, _____, to appear and answer completely all of the INTERROGATORIES attached within ten days after receipt, because:

1. On (date) _____, judgment was entered in favor of the _____
    and against the _____ in the amount of $ _____, with court costs
    in the amount of $ _____, for a total award of $ _____;
2. There remains due on this judgment the amount of $ _____, interest to date of $ _____,
    additional costs of $ _____, for a balance of $ _____;
3. Execution may presently issue on this judgment; and
4. Pursuant to C.R.C.P. 517 and 518, the judgment creditor is entitled to an order requiring the judgment debtor to
    appear and answer these interrogatories concerning the debtor's financial condition.

Date: _____   _____
                     Judgment Creditor

Subscribed under oath before me on:

Date: _____   _____
                     Clerk/Deputy

IT IS ORDERED:

1. That the judgment debtor, _____, APPEAR and ANSWER
    completely all of the INTERROGATORIES attached, pursuant to C.R.C.P. 517 and 518.
2. That these INTERROGATORIES be signed by the judgment debtor in full legal name, under penalty of perjury, in
    the presence of a notary public or clerk of court.
3. That these INTERROGATORIES be filed with the Clerk, and that the judgment debtor appear on
    (date) _____ (time) _____ at (location) _____
    _____.
4. That service of these INTERROGATORIES and this order be made by mailing copies to the judgment debtor, by
    certified mail, or as provided by C.R.C.P. 304.

Date: _____   _____
                     ☐ Judge ☐ Magistrate

I certify that a copy of this form and interrogatories
were mailed to the judgment debtor on:

Date: _____   _____
                     Clerk of Court/Deputy Clerk

JDF 252B R9/01 MOTION AND ORDER FOR INTERROGATORIES – LONG FORM (Page 1 of 6)

INTERROGATORIES TO JUDGMENT DEBTOR

Name of Judgment Debtor: _____. THESE INTERROGATORIES
MUST BE COMPLETELY ANSWERED AND FILED WITH THE CLERK OF THE _____
COUNTY COURT AT THE ADDRESS STATED ON PAGE 1 OF THIS FORM ON (date) _____
(time) _____. YOU MUST APPEAR ON THIS DATE.

**WARNING: FAILURE TO TRUTHFULLY AND COMPLETELY ANSWER ALL OF THESE QUESTIONS
AND RETURN THEM WITHIN TEN DAYS TO THE CLERK OF COUNTY COURT, SMALL
CLAIMS DIVISION, SHALL CAUSE A CITATION TO BE ISSUED FOR CONTEMPT OF
COURT. A FINDING OF CONTEMPT MAY BE CAUSE FOR A FINE OR JAIL SENTENCE.**

NOTE: YOU MAY PAY $ _____ (THE AMOUNT OF THE JUDGMENT TOGETHER WITH ANY
INTEREST AND COSTS) TO THE CLERK OF THE COURT WITHIN TEN DAYS INSTEAD OF
ANSWERING THESE QUESTIONS. IF YOU MAKE THE PAYMENT, THIS CASE WILL BE CLOSED.

1. What is your full legal name: _____
    List any other names you have been known by: _____
    Home address: _____
    Home phone number: _____ Work phone number: _____
    Date of birth: _____ Social Security Number: _____
    Drivers license number: _____ State: _____

2. State your full and correct business address: _____
    _____

    a. Do you rent or own the premises? _____
    b. State the full and correct name and address of your landlord. _____
        _____

    c. On what day of the month do you pay your rent? _____
    d. What is the amount of the deposit with your landlord? $_____

3. State your full and correct home address: _____
    _____

    a. Do you own or rent the premises? _____
    b. State the full and correct name and address of your landlord. _____
        _____

    c. On what day of the month do you pay your rent? _____
    d. What is the amount of the deposit with your landlord? _____

4. State the full and correct address of all real estate you own or have an interest in.

Address	City/County State
Address	City/County State
Address	City/County State
Address	City/County State

5. State the book and page number and other recording numbers of the deed or other instruments of such property.

Book/page number of deed	Book/page number of deed
Book/page number of deed	Book/page number of deed

JDF 252B R9/01 MOTION AND ORDER FOR INTERROGATORIES – LONG FORM (Page 2 of 6)

6. Are there any liens, mortgages, or encumbrances against any of the property referred to in No. 4? If so, give the full and correct name and address of the creditor of, and balance due on each.

Name	Address City/State	$_____ Amount owed
Name	Address City/State	$_____ Amount owed
Name	Address City/State	$_____ Amount owed
Name	Address City/State	$_____ Amount owed

7. Employment information:

The employer's/company's name: _____

Address of employer: _____

Phone number: _____ Supervisor's name: _____

You are paid: ☐ hourly $ _____ ☐ monthly $ _____ ☐ or your annual rate of pay you earn $ _____ ☐ you are paid commissions, the manner in which commissions are calculated are:

The days or days of the month on which you are paid: _____

8. If self-employed, do you own or have any interest in any inventory, supplies, machinery, equipment, or tools? If so, list each of them and whether they are paid for. If you owe money for any item, indicate how much for each item.

Type of Item	Paid YES or NO	If No, Amount owed
Type of Item	Paid YES or NO	If No, Amount owed
Type of Item	Paid YES or NO	If No, Amount owed
Type of Item	Paid YES or NO	If No, Amount owed

9. List the full and correct name and address of all banks and savings institutions you have:

Name of Bank Savings & Loan/Credit Union	Address/Location City/State	Account Number
Name of Bank Savings & Loan/Credit Union	Address/Location City/State	Account Number
Name of Bank Savings & Loan/Credit Union	Address/Location City/State	Account Number

10. Do you have any life, health, or other insurance with a cash surrender value or from which money is or will be due to you? If so, state the name and number of the policy and full and correct name and address of the insuring company.

Name of Insurance Company – Name of Agent	Address/Location City/State	Policy Number
Name of Insurance Company – Name of Agent	Address/Location City/State	Policy Number

11. Have you received any money judgments from any court within the past 12 months? If so, state the nature of the action, court location, case number, amount received and date judgment entered.

Nature of Action	Court Location	Case Number	Amount of Judgment	Date Ordered
Nature of Action	Court Location	Case Number	Amount of Judgment	Date Ordered
Nature of Action	Court Location	Case Number	Amount of Judgment	Date Ordered

12. Are you entitled to any refund on either or both of your last federal or state income tax returns?
    a. If so, what is the amount of the refund on each? _____
    b. Have you received any of this money as of this date? _____

13. State the description, amount, and location of any and all stocks, bonds, U.S. Savings Bonds, debentures, or other securities which you own or in which you have an interest.

Type of Stock/Bond/US Savings Bond	Location	$ _____ Amount
Type of Stock/Bond/US Savings Bond	Location	$ _____ Amount
Type of Stock/Bond/US Savings Bond	Location	$ _____ Amount
Type of Stock/Bond/US Savings Bond	Location	$ _____ Amount

14. State the amount and location of any cash you have on hand.

Location of Cash	$ _____ Amount
Location of Cash	$ _____ Amount

15. List and describe any and all automobiles, trucks or other motor vehicles owned by you, or vehicles in which you have an interest.

Type of Vehicle	$ _____ Estimated Value

    a. Are any of these vehicles used daily in your work? If so, identify _____
    b. Are any of these vehicles mortgaged? If so, state for what amount and the full and correct name and address of the mortgagee.

Name of Bank Savings & Loan/Credit Union	Address/Location City/State	Account Number
Name of Bank Savings & Loan/Credit Union	Address/Location City/State	Account Number

16. List and describe any and all livestock and crops you own or have an interest in, giving the location and present market value of each.

Type of Livestock/Crops	Location	$ _____ Estimated Value
Type of Livestock/Crops	Location	$ _____ Estimated Value

17. State the amount, description, and location of any and all other personal property you own or have an interest in including household furniture and fixtures, motorcycles, boats, photographic and electronic equipment, jewelry, and any other moveable property. If any of this property is mortgaged, state for what amount and the full and correct name and address of the mortgagee(s). (Use additional pages if necessary.)

Description	Location	$ _____ Estimated Value
Description	Location	$ _____ Estimated Value
Description	Location	$ _____ Estimated Value

18. State the full and correct name and address of any and all persons, firms, and/or corporations to whom you owe any money.

Name and address	$ _____ Amount

		$_____
Name and address		Amount

		$_____
Name and address		Amount

19. List and describe any and all rents, notes receivable, and accounts receivable, on an open account or otherwise, due or payable to you or in which you have an interest. State the full and correct name and address of the debtor and the amount due as of this date.

		$_____
List of Debtor	Address	Amount

		$_____
List of Debtor	Address	Amount

		$_____
List of Debtor	Address	Amount

		$_____
List of Debtor	Address	Amount

		$_____
List of Debtor	Address	Amount

20. State the full and correct address of the location of your financial books and records and, if you employ the services of a bookkeeper or accountant, the full correct name and address of such person. _____
_____
_____

21. What is the amount of your deposit with any utility company (gas, electric, water and sewer)?

		$_____
Description	Location	Estimated Value

		$_____
Description	Location	Estimated Value

22. What is the amount of your deposit with any telephone company? $ _____

23. For a period of one full year prior to the commencement of this legal action against you until the present, have you or your agents or employees, if any, closed out any savings, commercial, or other financial account which was in your name, individually or together with other people or business, in any bank or other financial institution? If so, for each of such closed accounts, state:
   a. The full and correct name and address of the bank or institution(s). _____
   _____
   b. The names on the account(s). _____
   c. The account number(s). _____
   d. The date on which the account(s) was/were opened. _____
   e. The date on which the account(s) was/were closed. _____

24. Supply a copy of your last federal income tax return.

I affirm/swear under the penalty of perjury that the above answers to these INTERROGATORIES are true, complete, and correct.

FALSE STATEMENT ARE PUNISHABLE AS PERJURY WHICH IS A FELONY.

Date: _____   _____
                                      Judgment Debtor

Subscribed and affirmed, or sworn to before me in the County of _____, State of _____, this _____ day of _____, 20 _____.

My commission expires: _____   _____
                                                       Notary Public/Deputy Clerk

JDF 252B R9/01   MOTION AND ORDER FOR INTERROGATORIES – LONG FORM (Page 5 of 6)

Case Name _____ v. _____ Case Number: _____

AFFIDAVIT OF SERVICE
(Must be returned to Court)

I served a copy of the foregoing Interrogatories, on the following:

Name   **Date**   **Place**

If the person on whom service was made is not the named party to be served, I served the Interrogatories:

☐   At the regular place of abode of the person to be served, by leaving the Notice with a person over the age of 18 years who regularly resides at the place of abode. (Identify relationship to defendant _____.)

☐   At the regular place of business of the person to be served, by leaving the Notice with that person's secretary, bookkeeper, chief clerk, office receptionist/assistant or partner. (Circle title of person who was served.)

☐   By leaving the Notice with a partner, limited partner, associate, manager, elected official, receptionist/assistant, bookkeeper or general agent of the partnership, limited liability company, or other non-corporate entity, which was to be served. (Circle title of person who was served.)

☐   By leaving the Notice with an officer, manager, receptionist/assistant, legal assistant, paid legal advisor or general agent, registered agent for service of process, stockholder or principal employee of the corporation that was to be served. (Circle title of person who was served.)

I am over the age of 18 years, and I am not an interested party in this matter.

I have charged the following fees for my services in this matter:

☐ Private process server
☐ Sheriff, _____ County
　 Fee $ _____ Mileage $ _____

_____
Signature of Process Server

_____
Name (Print or type)

Subscribed and affirmed, or sworn to before me in the County of _____, State of _____, this _____ day of _____, 20 _____.

My commission expires: _____

_____
Notary Public

CERTIFICATE OF SERVICE BY MAILING
(To be performed by Clerk within three days of filing)

I hereby certify that on (date) _____, I mailed a true and correct copy of the MOTION AND ORDER FOR INTERROGATORIES – LONG FORM, by placing it in the United States Mail, postage pre-paid to the Defendant(s) at the address(es) listed above.

_____
Clerk of Court/Deputy Clerk

☐ (If applicable) Plaintiff(s) notified of non-service on (date) _____. Clerk's Initials _____

REQUESTS TO SET ASIDE SMALL CLAIMS COURT JUDGMENTS

The rules of the Small Claims Court establish procedures which allow either the plaintiff or the defendant to ask the court later to set aside the ruling it made at the court hearing. This possibility arises when one of the parties is not present on the scheduled court date.

A defendant who did not appear at the hearing may complete form JDF 253, *Request to Set Aside Dismissal/ Default Judgment*, which is available from the clerk's office. The defendant will have to state the reason he was not at the trial, as well as the basis for his position that the money is not owed to the plaintiff. When this request is filed, a copy is mailed by the court to the plaintiff informing the plaintiff that the defendant will be making a motion to set aside the judgment in the same Small Claims Court at a given date and time of day. You must be prepared to appear and even go ahead with the trial if the defendant's motion is granted.

A plaintiff who did not appear at the hearing is probably in even worse shape than a defendant who did not appear. If the case was dismissed because the plaintiff was not there, the plaintiff may file form JDF 253. The plaintiff must also state why he was not present at the trial and why he thinks he can prevail in the case. Notice is then given to the defendant, who is informed that he must be present in court when the plaintiff argues his position, and that he should be prepared for trial should the plaintiff's request be granted.

Do not be alarmed by the prospect of having a judgment or dismissal set aside. These motions can only be filed within the thirty days immediately following the entry of judgment. The requesting party must also prove there was good cause why he could not appear at the trial when it was scheduled. This will have to be something extraordinary. Defendants' most common reason for seeking to set aside the judgment is that they were never served with the complaint. Be sure you can prove to the court that he was. Keep the green copy of the complaint with the Certificate of Personal Service for no less than a month after your trial date.

Small Claims Court, _____ County, Colorado

Court Address:

PLAINTIFF(S): _____

Address: _____

City/State/Zip: _____

Phone: Home _____ Work _____

v.

DEFENDANT(S): _____

Address: _____

City/State/Zip: _____

Phone: Home _____ Work _____

▲ **COURT USE ONLY** ▲

Case Number:

Division: Courtroom:

REQUEST TO SET ASIDE ☐ DISMISSAL ☐ DEFAULT JUDGMENT

UNDER PENALTIES OF PERJURY, I DECLARE THAT THESE STATEMENTS ARE TRUE AND CORRECT.

1. I/We _____, am the ☐ Plaintiff(s) ☐ Defendant(s) in above captioned case.
2. My claim against the Defendant(s) was/were dismissed on (date) _____.
   OR
   The Plaintiff(s) Judgment was/were entered against me on (date) _____.
3. I/We did not appear in Court on the ☐ date of the trial or the ☐ date of the entry of judgment because:

   _____
   _____

4. I/We believe I/we can provide the following facts to prove my/our case or to establish my/our defense:

   _____
   _____

Date: _____

_____
Signature

_____
Signature

ORDER

The Court upon review of Request to Set Aside ☐ Dismissal ☐ Default Judgment, ORDERS the following:

☐ Request **DENIED** ☐ Request **GRANTED**

☐ Request to be heard by the Court on (date) _____.

If after the request is heard and the Court finds that the request for dismissal/default judgment should be set aside, the Court

☐ will proceed immediately to trial at the conclusion of the hearing.

☐ will re-schedule the trial for another date.

THE PARTIES ARE ADVISED TO BRING WITH THEM ON THE SAID DATE ALL OF THE EVIDENCE AND WITNESSES NECESSARY FOR THE COURT TRIAL.

Date: _____

_____
☐ Judge ☐ Magistrate

CERTIFICATE OF MAILING

I hereby certify that on (date) _____, I mailed a true and correct copy of the REQUEST TO SET ASIDE DISMISSAL/DEFAULT JUDGMENT, by placing it in the United States Mail, postage pre-paid to the parties at the addresses listed above.

Date: _____

_____
Clerk of Court/Deputy Clerk

JDF 253 9/01 REQUEST TO SET ASIDE DISMISSAL/DEFAULT JUDGMENT

Courts generally do not grant these requests without a convincing explanation and a very compelling reason. Additionally, most parties who did not bother to appear the first time are not likely to ask for another hearing.

SAM'S CASE

When the magistrate finished announcing his ruling, Bob immediately blurted out, "But, your honor, this isn't fair!"

"Please, Mr. Lee," the magistrate said. "I have made my decision, and I think the judgment of the court is quite fair based on what I saw here today. You are free to appeal my ruling to the district court."

The magistrate then asked Bob if he could pay Sam the money right then and there. Bob replied that he could not. "But Mr. Lee," asked the magistrate, "didn't you say just a minute ago that you had the money?"

"Oh, sure, I *have* the money, your honor," Bob answered. "I just forgot to bring my checkbook to court today, that's all."

The magistrate glared at Bob for an extra second, and then turned to Sam and asked him if he would like the court to order Bob to fill out a set of interrogatories. Sam replied with an emphatic "yes." The magistrate turned back to Bob and told him to go to the clerk's office "right now" and get the interrogatories, answer them, and return to the courtroom when he was through. He advised Sam to wait for Bob to return.

Bob came back about twenty minutes later, and both he and Sam waited for the magistrate to call them back up front. When he did, he asked Bob for the completed interrogatories. The magistrate reviewed them, and then gave them to Sam for his review. Sam saw that Bob had not answered every single question completely, but also noted that the interrogatories contained information about Bob's job, real estate, and bank accounts, so he told the magistrate that he was satisfied with the answers. The magistrate thanked Bob and Sam, and sent them on their way.

As they left, Sam asked Bob if he could pay the money, offering to drop the court costs if Bob would just pay the $1,000. Bob told Sam he did not really have the money now, but that he was expecting a "big payment" soon. Bob said he would be in touch.

Bob's reply made Sam check again to make sure he still had the interrogatories with him before he left the courthouse.

APPEALS

As with any other court case, parties retain the right to appeal a judgment that may have been entered against them to a higher court. Unless the parties have agreed in advance of the trial to be bound by the ruling of the Small Claims Court, either the plaintiff or the defendant may appeal. There will be no new trial in the Small Claims Court. Rather, an appeal can be filed in the District Court of the same county. This appeal must be filed within fifteen days of the date judgment was entered. The Small Claims Court may ask to retain any exhibits presented during the trial for use by the court hearing the appeal.

The District Court is an entirely different animal than the Small Claims Court. All formal legal rules and procedures are followed, and most parties are represented by an attorney. You should definitely consider retaining a lawyer if you or the other party has decided to appeal the case. If you are the party interested in an appeal, an attorney can assist you with the technicalities of preparing and filing an appeal.

Chapter 11: Collecting Your Money

FOCUSING ON YOUR ULTIMATE GOAL

Now that you have obtained a judgment in Small Claims Court against the person who owes you money, you are ready for the final step in the process: transferring money from the debtor's control to yours. If you have been able to get the defendant to hand over what he owes you prior to any attempts at forcing him to do so, you can stop now. You have achieved your ultimate goal, which was to get the defendant to pay you what you were rightfully owed.

Unfortunately, many losing defendants in Small Claims Court are not so forthcoming. If your debtor refuses to pay up after a judgment is entered against him, you must take action to make him pay the debt. It has been said that getting a judgment in Small Claims Court is the easy part; collecting your money is where it really becomes difficult. In many instances, this is true. There are, however, a number of legal mechanisms you can use to increase the chances that your claim will be paid by the debtor.

An important point to keep in mind now that you are ready to enforce collection of your judgment is that the court does not guarantee that you will collect your money. The entire small claims process exists merely as a path you can take to try to collect what is owed you. Courts do not compel or demand that civil judgments be paid.

It is time again to invoke the notion of perseverance. Your ability and willingness to stick to the case may have already been severely tested by the process of filing a small claims case, successfully serving the other party, preparing for the trial, and actually going through with the court appearance. Even if you won, you might be tempted to throw in the towel when your defendant says something like, "Good luck gettin' any money outta me, pal!," as he passes you in the hallway outside the courtroom after the trial. Maybe you should just be content with a moral victory, right?

Wrong. If you quit now, the defendant wins, even if you are holding a piece of paper saying you won the case. **Now** is the time to steel your resolve and focus on prevailing in the last phase of the game. While collection is far from assured, there are tools at your disposal which can be used successfully against many debtors. These are methods used by professionals in the field of debt collection everyday, and they can be used by you, too.

If you don't receive payment from the defendant immediately after the hearing, you are free to pursue the remedies described in this chapter as soon as the judgment is entered. You need not wait for the expiration of the time periods during which the defendant can file a motion to set aside the judgment or file an appeal. The court, in its discretion, can grant a stay of execution pending the outcome of such motions filed by the defendant. If this happens, you will be informed by the court, and you may not pursue collection until the defendant's motion has been heard.

A WORD OF WARNING before you start to collect on the judgment. The law provides certain ways to assist you in the collection of your money. Once you get a judgment, you are free to pursue these debt collection methods. You may not, however, harass, annoy, or threaten the debtor or his family. Avoid the temptation to constantly call the debtor's house at strange hours to ask him why he has not paid you yet.

GATHERING INFORMATION – AGAIN

Obtaining accurate information regarding your debtor is a vital prerequisite to collecting on a Small Claims Court judgment. You should have taken the first step in the process of collecting information by having the court compel the debtor to answer the interrogatories described in the previous chapter. This is the single best source of data about the debtor's assets and employment you are likely to acquire.

The interrogatories are not the sole source of information, however. If, for whatever reason, you have not been successful in getting the completed interrogatories from the debtor—or even if you have—you can gain valuable information from other sources. Some of this information may be right under your very nose.

Probably the single most important piece of information in most cases is the employment of the debtor. If you still do not know where the debtor works, try asking someone who knows the defendant about this. You need not let on why you want to know. If you think you know where he works, but are not sure, call the personnel office of the business. They may well be able to confirm that the debtor is in fact employed there.

Be creative when attempting to obtain information about the debtor's assets. Begin with documents you may already have in your possession. If the defendant has paid you any money at all by check, either before or after you won your judgment, you can get valuable information about where the defendant banks as well as account numbers from these checks. Contact your bank. You may have, or easily be able to find out, the license plate numbers of vehicles owned by the defendant. Landlords and other creditors may have rental forms, credit applications, and other paperwork in which the debtor listed some assets. Check with any such documents you may have or have access to.

There are also ways to determine if the debtor owns real estate. The easiest way to do this is to call the County Assessor's Office in a county where you suspect the debtor owns property and ask them to perform a check for you. If the debtor does own property in that county, the assessor will tell you and give you the address. Record this information accurately. You can also try this in any Colorado county, even if you have no idea if the debtor owns any property in that county.

You can also have the assessor confirm your suspicion about whether the defendant owns a certain property. Contact the Assessor's Office and provide them with an address in that county. The assessor can tell you who is listed in their records as the owner of that property. This can be very helpful in determining whether a debtor owns or rents his home.

After you have gathered all the information you can about the debtor's assets and employment, you are ready to try one of the following remedies to collect on your judgment.

GARNISHING THE DEBTOR'S WAGES OR SALARY

If your debtor has a steady job, and you know where he works, using a garnishment on that person's pay is the simplest and most effective way of collecting your money. It is the enforcement tool used most effectively by people who have prevailed in Small Claims Court.

However, a garnishment of this type works only against those debtors who are regularly employed. It cannot be used against people who, for whatever reason, do not hold jobs. It is generally not useful against people who do work but are paid in cash, or those who get their financial support from their parents or some other kind person. The debtor's job or source of income must be in Colorado for you to serve a Colorado garnishment. Finally, the debtor must be a real person, not a corporation, partnership or association for you to use this type of garnishment. You may not garnish a corporation's "pay" using a wage or salary garnishment.

The concept of a garnishment is not complicated. The idea is that, because you are owed money by the debtor, you can go to someone else who owes the debtor money and intercept that money before this third party pays the debtor. The laws of garnishment set up a mechanism with certain rules and procedures which allow you to intercept the debtor's money before it lands in his pocket.

Begin the process by obtaining form No. 1140, *Writ of Continuing Garnishment;* form No. 1141, *Calculation of the Amount of Exempt Earnings;* and form No. 1142, *Objection to Calculation of the Amount of Exempt Earnings.* You can get these forms from Bradford Publishing Company or an office supply store which sells legal forms, or possibly from the court clerk's office. (For information on ordering forms, see Appendix B)

You will need an original and 4 copies of the form 1140: the original for the Court, two that are served on the garnishee, one for the process server (who will fill out the Return of Service and give to the Court as proof of service), and one for your records.

Form 1141 is an 8½ x 11" form that has two Calculation forms on it with perforations between each form. Each form looks much like a money receipt. The garnishee will be required to attach one of these forms each time the judgment debtor is paid and a payment is sent to the Court. You may want to send the garnishee enough forms to cover the 180 days that this writ will be in effect. If the debtor is paid every other week, that would require approximately 13 sheets of two.

☐ County Court ☐ District Court **❶** _____ County, Colorado Court address: **Plaintiff(s)/Petitioner(s):** **❷** v. **Defendant(s)/Respondent(s):** **❸** Judgment Creditor's Attorney or Judgment Creditor (Name and Address): **❹** Phone Number: E-mail: FAX Number: Atty. Reg. #:	 ▲ COURT USE ONLY ▲ Case Number: Division: Courtroom:

WRIT OF CONTINUING GARNISHMENT

Judgment Debtor's name, last known address, other identifying information: ___ **❺** _____

_____

1. Original Amount of Judgment $ ___ **❼** ___   DATE SUIT WAS
   a. Judgment Entered ___ **❻** _____ (date)   COMMENCED: **⓮**
   b. Effective Garnishment Period   (Mark Appropriate Box)
      ☐ 90 days (Judgment entered prior to August 8, 2001)   ☐ Prior to May 1, 1991
   ❽ ☐ 180 days (Judgment entered on or after August 8, 2001)   ☐ On or After May 1, 1991
2. Plus any Interest Due on Judgment (___ **❾** ___ % per annum) $ ___ **❿** ___
3. Taxable Costs (including estimated cost of service of this Writ) $ ___ **⓫** ___
4. Less any Amount Paid $ ___ **⓬** ___
5. Principal Balance/Total Amount Due and Owing $ ___ **⓭** ___

I affirm that I am authorized to act for the Judgment Creditor and this is a correct statement as of _____.
                                                                                              (Date)

Subscribed under oath before me on ___ **⓯** ___   ___ **⓱** ___
                                                           (Print Judgment Creditor's Name)
___ **⓰** _____   Address: ___ **⓱** ___
Notary Public or Deputy Clerk

My Commission Expires: ___ **⓰** ___   By: ___ **⓲** ___
                                                   Signature (Type Name, Title, Address & Phone)

WRIT OF CONTINUING GARNISHMENT

THE PEOPLE OF THE STATE OF COLORADO to the Sheriff of any Colorado County, or to any person over the age of 18 years who is not a party to this action:
   You are directed to serve TWO COPIES of this Writ of Continuing Garnishment upon ___ **⓳** _____
_____.

Garnishee, with proper return of service to be made to the Court.

TO THE GARNISHEE:
YOU ARE SUMMONED AS GARNISHEE IN THIS ACTION AND ORDERED:
   a. To answer the following questions under oath and file your answers with the Clerk of the Court and mail a completed copy with

(Continued on Reverse Side)

No. 1140. Rev. 8-01. WRIT OF CONTINUING GARNISHMENT (C.R.C.P. Form 26) (Page 1 of 3)
 Bradford Publishing, 1743 Wazee St., Denver, CO 80202 — 303-292-2500 — www.bradfordpublishing.com — 7-01 your answers to the Judgment Creditor or attorney no less than 5 nor more than 10 days following the time you pay the Judgment Debtor for the first time following service of this Writ, or 40 days following service of this Writ upon you, whichever is less. **YOUR FAILURE TO ANSWER THIS WRIT OF CONTINUING GARNISHMENT MAY RESULT IN THE ENTRY OF A DEFAULT AGAINST YOU.**

b. To pay any nonexempt earnings to the party designated in "e" below no less than 5 nor more than 10 days following each time you pay the Judgment Debtor during the Effective Garnishment Period of this Writ and attach a copy of the Calculation of the Amount of Exempt Earnings used (the Calculation under "Questions to be Answered by Garnishee" should be used for the first pay period, and one of the multiple Calculation forms included with this Writ should be used for all subsequent pay periods).

c. To deliver a copy of this Writ, together with the Calculation of the Amount of Exempt Earnings and a blank Objection to Calculation of the Amount of Exempt Earnings form, the first time you pay the Judgment Debtor.

d. To deliver to the Judgment Debtor a copy of each subsequent Calculation of the Amount of Exempt Earnings each time you pay the Judgment Debtor for earnings subject to this Writ.

20 e. **MAKE CHECK PAYABLE TO:** ☐ Clerk of the _____ Court ☐ Judgment Creditor named above **AND MAIL TO:** ☐ CLERK OF THE COURT ☐ JUDGMENT CREDITOR ☐ JUDGMENT CREDITOR'S ATTORNEY

Name and _____

Address _____

PLEASE PUT THE CASE NUMBER (shown above) ON THE FRONT OF THE CHECK.

CLERK OF THE COURT   By: _____
                                            Deputy Clerk

                                      Date: _____

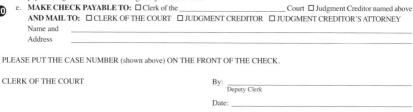

NOTICE TO GARNISHEE

a. This Writ applies to all nonexempt earnings owed or owing during the Effective Garnishment Period shown on Line 1b on the front of this Writ or until you have paid to the party, designated in paragraph 'e' on the front of this Writ, the amount shown on Line 5 on the front of this Writ, whichever occurs first. **However, if you have already been served with a Writ of Continuing Garnishment or Writ of Garnishment for Child Support, this new Writ is effective for the Effective Garnishment Period after any prior Writ terminates.**

b. "EARNINGS" INCLUDES ALL FORMS OF COMPENSATION FOR PERSONAL SERVICES. Also read "Notice to Judgment Debtor" below.

c. In no case may you withhold any amount greater than the amount on Line 5 on the front of this Writ.

QUESTIONS TO BE ANSWERED BY GARNISHEE

The following questions MUST be answered by you under oath:

a. On the date and time this Writ of Continuing Garnishment was served upon you, did you owe or do you anticipate owing any of the following to the Judgment Debtor within the Effective Garnishment Period (see Line 1b on the front of this Writ)? (Mark appropriate box(es))

   1. ☐ WAGES/SALARY/COMMISSIONS/BONUS/OTHER COMPENSATION FOR PERSONAL SERVICES (Earnings)

   2. ☐ Health, Accident or Disability Insurance Funds or Payments

   3. ☐ Pension or Retirement Benefits (for suits commenced prior to 5/1/91 ONLY — check front of Writ for date)

   If you marked any box above, indicate how the Judgment Debtor is paid:

   ☐ weekly ☐ biweekly ☐ semimonthly ☐ monthly ☐ other

The Judgment Debtor will be paid on the following dates during the Effective Garnishment Period (see Line 1b on the front of this Writ): _____

b. Are you under one or more of the following writs of garnishment? (Mark appropriate box(es))

   4. ☐ Writ of Continuing Garnishment (Expected Termination Date _____)

   5. ☐ Writ of Garnishment for Support (Expected Termination Date _____)

c. If you marked Box 1 and you did NOT mark either Box 4 or 5, complete the Calculation below for the "First Pay Period" following receipt of this Writ. If you marked either Box 4 or 5, you must complete Calculations beginning with the first pay period following termination of the prior writ(s).

d. If you marked Box 2 or 3 and you did NOT mark either Box 4 or 5, complete the Calculation below for the "First Pay Period" following receipt of this Writ. If you marked either Box 4 or 5, you must complete Calculations beginning with the first pay period following termination of the prior writ(s). However, there are a number of total exemptions, and you should seek legal advice about such exemptions. IF THE EARNINGS ARE TOTALLY EXEMPT, PLEASE MARK BOX 6 BELOW:

6. ☐ THE EARNINGS ARE TOTALLY EXEMPT BECAUSE _____

CALCULATION OF THE AMOUNT OF EXEMPT EARNINGS (First Pay Period)

Gross Earnings for the First Pay Period from _____ thru _____ $ _____

Less Deductions Required by Law (For Example, Withholding Taxes, FICA) – $ _____

Disposable Earnings (Gross Earnings less Deductions) = $ _____

Less Statutory Exemption (Use Exemption Chart Below) – $ _____

Net Amount Subject to Garnishment = $ _____

Less Wage/Income Assignment(s) During Pay Period (If Any) – $ _____

AMOUNT TO BE WITHHELD AND PAID = $ _____

EXEMPTION CHART	PAY PERIOD	AMOUNT EXEMPT IS GREATER OF	
	Weekly	30 × Federal Minimum Hourly Wage ($154.50) or 75% of Disposable Earnings	Amounts in parentheses based upon Federal Minimum Hourly Wage of $5.15.
	Bi-weekly	60 × Federal Minimum Hourly Wage ($309.00) or 75% of Disposable Earnings	
	Semi-monthly	65 × Federal Minimum Hourly Wage ($334.75) or 75% of Disposable Earnings	
	Monthly	130 × Federal Minimum Hourly Wage ($669.50) or 75% of Disposable Earnings	

I affirm that I am authorized to act for the Garnishee, the above answers are true and correct, and I have delivered a copy of this Writ, together with the Calculation of the Amount of Exempt Earnings and a blank Objection to Calculation of the Amount of Exempt Earnings form to the Judgment Debtor at the time earnings were paid for the "First Pay Period" (if earnings were paid).

Subscribed under oath before me on _____ (Date)

_____
(Notary Public)

My Commission Expires: _____

Name of Garnishee (Print) _____

Address: _____

Phone Number _____
Name of Person Answering (Print) _____

Signature of Person Answering _____

NOTICE TO JUDGMENT DEBTOR

a. The Garnishee may only withhold nonexempt earnings from the amount due you, but in no event more than the amount on Line 5 on the front of this Writ, UNLESS YOUR EARNINGS ARE TOTALLY EXEMPT, in which case NO EARNINGS CAN BE WITHHELD. You may wish to contact a lawyer who can explain your rights.

b. If you disagree with the amount withheld, you must talk with the Garnishee within 5 days after being paid.

c. If you cannot settle the disagreement with the Garnishee, you may complete and file the attached Objection with the Clerk of the Court issuing this Writ within 10 days after being paid. YOU MUST USE THE FORM ATTACHED or a copy of it.

d. You are entitled to a court hearing on your written objection.

e. Your employer cannot fire you because your earnings have been garnished. If your employer discharges you in violation of your legal rights, you may, within 90 days, bring a civil action for the recovery of wages lost because you were fired and for an order requiring that you be reinstated. Damages will not exceed six weeks' wages and attorney's fees.

RETURN OF SERVICE

STATE OF COLORADO _____ County of _____

I, _____, affirm that I served two copies of the Writ of Continuing Garnishment, together with a blank Objection to Calculation of the Amount of Exempt Earnings on _____ (date), at _____ (time), by _____.

Subscribed under oath before me on _____ (Date)

_____
(Notary Public)

_____
(Signature)

My Commission Expires: _____

Service Fee $ _____

No. 1140. (C.R.C.P. Form 26) (Page 3 of 3)

COMPLETING THE WRIT OF CONTINUING GARNISHMENT (FORM NO. 1140)

The Writ of Continuing Garnishment should be completed as follows:

1. Check to box for County Court, and write the name of the county where your case has been heard.
2. List your name as it appears on your initial complaint.
3. List the debtor's name and any business name here as they appear on the original complaint.
4. List your name and address here. If you have hired an attorney to help you collect, then list the attorney's name instead. Also list your—or the attorney's—telephone number, fax number, and e-mail address.
5. Repeat the debtor's name, then list his address or addresses, any business names, phone numbers, and Social Security numbers, if you know them.
6. List the date the judgment was entered by the court.
7. List the amount you were awarded by the court, not including costs of filing or service.
8. If your judgment was entered by the court on or after August 8, 2001, check the box by "180 days". For judgments entered before that date, check the "90 days" box. Writs of garnishment in older cases may be in effect for only 90 days.
9. Insert here the percentage rate of any interest. Interest is usually eight percent, unless a court orders that it be otherwise. This could occur if there was a contract between the plaintiff and the defendant which included a different rate of interest.
10. Interest is compounded, on the unpaid amount, once a year from the date of the judgment. If your judgment is less than one year old, do not list an amount here. Also, you are not required to ask for interest. If you are not sure what this amount should be, you may leave this blank.
11. Add all your costs in the case and list the total here. Include filing fees and service costs for the complaint, the filing fee for the writ of garnishment, and the amount you estimate it will cost you to serve the writ of garnishment. Do not include items such as lost wages,

costs of parking at the courthouse, or phone bills incurred in pursuing the case or the garnishment.

12. List any amount toward your judgment the defendant has already paid you, either voluntarily or involuntarily, including the money received from other garnishments.

13. List the net total the debtor owes you at this moment after adding the amount of interest and costs to your original judgment amount and subtracting what you have already received from the debtor toward the judgment.

14. Check the appropriate box.

15. Enter the date that you sign this form in front of the notary or deputy clerk.

16. Have a deputy clerk or another notary public fill this in for you.

17. Type your name and address in these spaces. If the judgment creditor is a business, type the name of the business and the business address.

18. Sign this form in the presence of the deputy clerk or other notary and type your phone number below it. If you are signing on behalf of a business, type your name, title and phone number below your signature. Type the address if it is different from number 17.

19. List the name and address of the employer on whom the garnishment will be served. This employer or other third party is the "garnishee." You can call the appropriate city or county sales tax licensing office to determine the correct name of the business. If the employer is a sole proprietorship, use the person's name and the "d/b/a" abbreviation, as in "Max Smith, d/b/a Max's Chow House."

20. The court clerk will complete this section of the writ.

After you have completed the front of the *Writ of Continuing Garnishment* form, take the original and three copies to the court clerk's office. The clerk will then issue the writ after you pay a fee of $15. (Note: This fee is subject to change.)

Next, take the three copies of the writ to the sheriff's office in the county where the employer is located, or the county where the employer's registered agent is located if the employer is a corporation. A corporate employer must be served via the registered agent. Call the Secretary of State's Office at (303) 894-2251 to get the name and address of the registered agent. You must provide the sheriff with the correct information regarding who the garnishee is, be it a registered agent for a corporation or the owner of a sole proprietorship. You must also give the sheriff the blank copy of form 1142, *Objection to the Calculation of Exempt Earnings,* and at least one sheet of form 1141, *Calculation of the Amount of Exempt Earnings.* The Objection form will be passed on to the debtor by the employer.

If the defendant is paid by a company which is based out of state, you can still serve that corporation's Colorado registered agent. However, if there is no registered agent or business office in Colorado, you probably can't garnish the defendant's wages.

As with other instances involving service of process, you are free to use a private process server.

After being served, the employer-garnishee must complete pages 2 and 3 of the *Writ of Continuing Garnishment* by answering the questions it contains. The questions addressed to the garnishee include space for a calculation of the amount the employer must take from the debtor's pay. The garnishee must give the debtor employee a copy of the writ and the blank Objection Form. He must return the completed form to the Court between five and ten days following the date the judgment debtor receives earnings for the next pay period, or within forty days after the writ was served on the employer, whichever time period is less. If you enclose a self-addressed stamped envelope, the Garnishee will send a copy of the Writ back to you. The garnishee must pay the clerk of the court the withheld amount no less than five and no more than ten days after the debtor's pay day. On all subsequent pay periods, the garnishee must include a *Calculation of the Amount of Exempt Earnings* form, which shows how the garnishment calculation was done each time a withholding is made.

The general rule is that the creditor is entitled to twenty-five percent of what the debtor is paid in every paycheck. However, the amount from which the twenty-five percent is calculated is first reduced by any deductions the debtor is required by law to have taken from his pay, such as amounts for income tax withholding and social security. This then yields the amount of the debtor's "disposable earnings," from which the twenty-five percent for the creditor is taken.

When the next pay day for the debtor comes around, the garnishee must intercept this amount, up to the total amount due, from the debtor on behalf of the creditor. The garnishee then sends it to the Clerk of Court, who notes the amount paid, and sends it to the creditor.

OBJECTION!

To make matters even more complicated, the debtor is allowed to object to the garnishment of his pay. He can claim some or all of his pay is exempt from garnishment, and thus less, or none, of it can be taken by the employer and given to you. The debtor must first try to press his case with his employer. If this does not resolve the matter, he may file a formal objection with the court stating why he feels the amount withheld is not correct. He may not, however, argue about the merits of the case which resulted in the judgment being entered against him. It is permissible for the debtor to go to his employer and say "I think your math was wrong when you calculated the amount of the garnishment," but it is not acceptable for him to try to stop his employer from proceeding with the garnishment by saying that "I got railroaded by the court on this. I don't really owe that guy any money."

If the debtor does file a formal objection, you will receive a copy of form No. 1142, *Objection to the Calculation of the Amount of Exempt Earnings*. A court hearing may be held if pressed by the debtor. The only point at issue will be the amount of the garnishment based on the calculation. The validity of your judgment is not open to scrutiny at such a hearing. However, you will not receive any payments from the garnishment until the matter is resolved.

A writ of continuing garnishment served on an employer is good for 180 days, or until the amount listed on line five of the garnishment form is paid off. The employer must make a deduction for your garnishment from the debtor's pay on every pay day that falls within this 180 day period, regardless of whether the debtor is paid weekly, biweekly, or monthly. If the garnishment is successful, you will receive a number of checks from the court in the next six months.

(C.R.C.P. No. 28)

☐ County Court ☐ District Court _____ County, Colorado Court address: **Petitioner(s)/Plaintiff(s):** v. **Respondent(s)/Defendant(s):** Judgment Debtor's Attorney or Judgment Debtor (Name and Address): Phone Number: E-mail: Fax Number: Atty. Reg. #:	 ▲ COURT USE ONLY ▲ Case Number: Division: Courtroom:

OBJECTION TO CALCULATION OF THE AMOUNT OF EXEMPT EARNINGS

NOTICE TO JUDGMENT DEBTOR:
THIS FORM MUST BE USED TO OBJECT TO THE CALCULATION OF EXEMPT EARNINGS

My Name _____ Phone _____
Address _____
                            (Street, City, State, Zip Code)

1.   I object to the Garnishee's Calculation of the Amount of Exempt Earnings because
I BELIEVE THE CORRECT CALCULATION IS:

Gross Earnings for My Pay Period from _____ thru _____ $_____
Less Deductions Required by Law (For Example, Withholding Taxes, FICA)   – $_____
Disposable Earnings (Gross Earnings Less Deductions)   = $_____
Less Statutory Exemption (Use Exemption Chart on Writ)   – $_____
Net Amount Subject to Garnishment   = $_____
Less Wage/Income Assignment(s) During Pay Period (If Any)   – $_____
AMOUNT WHICH SHOULD HAVE BEEN WITHHELD   = $_____

OR

2.   The earnings garnished are pension or retirement benefits/deferred compensation/health, accident or disability insurance
AND THEY ARE TOTALLY EXEMPT BECAUSE: _____

I understand that I must make a good faith effort to resolve my dispute with the Garnishee.
I ☐ have   ☐ have not attempted to resolve this dispute with the Garnishee.
Name of Person I Talked to: _____
Position: _____
Phone Number: _____

TO GARNISHEE: BY FILING THIS OBJECTION, YOU ARE DIRECTED TO SEND MY NONEXEMPT EARNINGS TO THE COURT AT THE
ADDRESS NOTED INSTEAD OF TO THE PARTY DESIGNATED IN PARAGRAPH 'e', ON THE FRONT OF THE WRIT OF CONTINUING
GARNISHMENT. THE COURT WILL HOLD MY NONEXEMPT EARNINGS IN ITS REGISTRY UNTIL MY OBJECTION IS RESOLVED.

I certify that I mailed a copy of this document by certified mail, return receipt requested, to:

THE GARNISHEE   JUDGMENT CREDITOR OR ATTORNEY

Address: _____   Address: _____
_____CO _____   _____CO _____

Subscribed under oath on _____   _____
                       Date   Signature of Judgment Debtor
_____   My Commission Expires: _____
Notary Public/Deputy Clerk

No. 1142. Rev. 8-01. OBJECTION TO CALCULATION OF THE AMOUNT OF EXEMPT EARNINGS
Bradford Publishing, 1743 Wazee St., Denver, CO 80202 — (303) 292-2500 — www.bradfordpublishing.com

When the 180 days have passed, you must go through the entire process again to keep the garnishment going. This means completing a new writ, filing it with the court, and serving it on the garnishee. When filling out subsequent garnishments, be sure to include any new filing and service fees on line three and also remember to subtract money received since the last garnishment was filed on line four. While filing a new writ of garnishment may seem like a hassle, it is definitely worth your while to keep repeating the garnishment process as long as you have been receiving money using this method.

You may hear from the garnishee that there are already garnishments in place against the debtor which take the entire amount of the debtor's pay available for garnishments. If this is the case, your garnishment will kick in when these other garnishments expire. Your garnishment will then be good for 180 days from the date it goes into effect, not the date it was issued. Keep in mind, however, that a garnishment or wage assignment for child support always takes priority over other types of garnishments.

If the employer does not answer a writ of garnishment you have properly served, ask the court clerk for a default judgment against the employer. This could result in the employer also being liable for the amount of your claim.

Perhaps you will encounter the situation where the debtor works for a small business where the debtor's best friend is the boss and owner. After you serve the writ, you hear from the employer that the debtor does not work there, so the employer does not honor the garnishment. However, you know the garnishee is reluctant to take money from his friend, the debtor. If the employer answers that the debtor does not work for that business, but you know that he does, you may file something called a "traverse." There is no form for a traverse, but it is a simple document you can type on your own. List all the relevant case information, including your case number and the names of the parties and the garnishee. Then state that you served a writ of garnishment on the employer and what the employer said in response. Finally, in your own words, tell the court why you think the employer is incorrect. Say, for example, that you have seen the debtor working at the business. File this document with the court, and ask for a hearing. The employer will be called upon to explain his position to a judge, and will probably back down.

The law states that employers may not fire an employee solely because a creditor of the employee has served a garnishment on the employer. If this does occur, the employee is entitled to bring an action for lost wages, attorney's fees, and reinstatement. However, even though employees have this legal protection, many are uncomfortable with the idea of the boss knowing that the employee owes someone a debt based on a court judgment. For this reason, some debtors will attempt to settle the case with you when a garnishment is put into place.

Should the debtor come to you wanting to settle the debt after you have filed a writ of garnishment, take it as a good sign. Ask for the full amount first, and only settle for a large part of the total amount in return for stopping the garnishment. Protect yourself by making copies of any checks you receive from the debtor, so you can capture the bank account information.

If you wish to stop the garnishment, it can be "suspended" by the creditor by filing a written agreement with the court. A copy of this written agreement must also be delivered by you to the garnishee. A suspension does not extend the ninety day effective period of the garnishment.

As a judgment creditor, you are also required to refund to the Clerk of the Court any funds you receive in excess of the amount due in line five of the garnishment form, should the garnishee inadvertently send you too much money. If you find yourself in this situation, return the extra money and consider yourself lucky that your claim has been paid in full.

GARNISHING THE DEBTOR'S BANK ACCOUNT

Another enforcement tool you can use against the debtor in your case is a garnishment of funds in bank accounts belonging to the debtor. Again, you seek to intercept funds held by a third party on behalf of the debtor, before the debtor can withdraw them. This time, instead of an employer, the third party is a bank or other financial institution.

Begin by obtaining form No. 1143, *Writ of Garnishment with Notice of Exemption and Pending Levy* and form No. 1144, *Claim of Exemption to Writ of Garnishment.* Both are available at Bradford Publishing Company in Denver, an office

supply store which carries legal forms or possibly the court
clerk's office.

This type of writ is often referred to as a "bank garnishment" because it is frequently used by creditors to intercept
funds in a debtor's bank account. You will need an original plus
5 copies of the writ for the following: the original for the Court,
one for the bank, one for the process server or sheriff, and one
for your records. If funds are found in the account, a copy of the
answers that, yes, it does have money belonging to the Writ and
the Objection form will then be served on the debtor. The person
serving these forms will need a copy of the writ so that he can fill
out the Return of Service on the back and send it to the court.

The information included on this *Writ of Garnishment* is
similar to that used in the writ for garnishing wages. You can list
the judgment debtor's bank account number when the form
asks for identifying information about the debtor.

On the bottom half of the form, list the name of the bank,
as well as its address, as the garnishee. It is not enough to say
"Wells Fargo Bank." You must determine in advance whether
the bank you have in mind is a branch bank. Wells Fargo banks,
for example, are branch banks. This means that you can serve
the writ at the main bank in downtown Denver or a specific
branch. However, some banks which are affiliated and are even
portrayed in advertisements as being the same are actually
legally separate institutions. If they are separate, you must serve
the specific bank where the debtor has an account. You cannot
just serve the Second National Bank of Colorado at its Capitol
Hill location when the debtor's account is with the Second
National Bank of Colorado in Wheat Ridge if those two banks
are separate entities. One way to determine whether banks are
merely branches or are truly separate is to call the bank and ask
if you can make deposits at any of its locations. If you can, it is
probably a series of branch banks. If, however, a holding
company controls legally distinguishable banks, the answer will
be no. Generally, all savings and loan institutions are operated
as branches.

After you complete the form, have the court clerk issue it,
and take it to the sheriff or other process server. Refer to the
service of process rules discussed in Chapter 4. A writ of
Garnishment may NOT be served by certified mail. Only one

(C.R.C.P. 29)

☐ County Court   ☐ District Court

_____ County, Colorado

Court Address:

Plaintiff(s)/Petitioner(s):

v.

Defendant(s)/Respondent(s):

Judgment Creditor's Attorney or Judgment Creditor (Name and Address):

▲   COURT USE ONLY   ▲

Case Number:

Phone Number: E-mail:

FAX Number: Atty. Reg. #:   Division: Courtroom:

WRIT OF GARNISHMENT WITH NOTICE OF EXEMPTION AND PENDING LEVY

Judgment Debtor's name, last known address, other identifying information: _____

_____

1. Original Amount of Judgment Entered _____ $ _____
    (date)

2. Plus any Interest Due on Judgment (_____ % per annum)   + $ _____
3. Taxable Costs (including estimated cost of service of this Writ)   + $ _____
4. Less any Amount Paid   − $ _____
5. Principal Balance/Total Amount Due and Owing   = $ _____

I affirm that I am authorized to act for the Judgment Creditor and this is a correct statement as of _____.
    (date)

Print Judgment

Subscribed under oath before me on _____   Creditor's Name _____
    (Date)   Address: _____

_____

_____

Notary Public or Deputy Clerk

By: _____
    Signature (Type Name, Title, Address and Phone)

My Commission Expires: _____

WRIT OF GARNISHMENT WITH NOTICE OF EXEMPTION AND PENDING LEVY

THE PEOPLE OF THE STATE OF COLORADO to the Sheriff of any Colorado County, or to any person over the age of 18 years who is not a party to this action:
You are directed to serve a copy of this Writ of Garnishment upon _____
_____, Garnishee, with proper return of service to be made to the Court.

(See Reverse Side)

No. 1143. Rev. 8-01.   **WRIT OF GARNISHMENT WITH NOTICE OF EXEMPTION AND PENDING LEVY (Page 1 of 3)**

Bradford Publishing, 1743 Wazee St., Denver, CO 80202 — (303) 292-2500 — www.bradfordpublishing.com

copy of the writ needs to be served on the bank. You can attach a self-addressed stamped envelope to the writ, and the bank will return its answers by mail directly to you.

Following service, wait a week or two, and then go to the court to check on the bank's response—or check your mailbox for the bank's reply in your self-addressed stamped envelope. On the rear side of the writ is space for the bank to answer questions regarding the debtor's assets held by the bank. If the bank debtor, the bank will seize all money it has in the name of the debtor, up to the amount of your claim.

Your next step is to serve a copy of the *Writ of Garnishment* and the *Claim of Exemption* forms on the debtor via the sheriff or a private process server. The debtor then has 10 days to make a claim of exemption to stop the seizure. This is done by filing the *Claim of Exemption* form with the court. The debtor can claim that all or part of the money seized by the bank is exempt from a writ of garnishment because it is made up of funds which originated from items found in the list on the back of the garnishment form. For example, he can claim the money in his bank account is from workers' compensation benefits, life insurance benefits, or the sale of a homestead property. Money from these sources is not garnishable.

The debtor has ten days to file his exemption claim with the court. You will receive a copy of the form from the debtor. A court hearing will be scheduled for the debtor to explain to the court why this money is exempt from garnishment. If the court does not allow the debtor's claim, or if the debtor does not appear at the hearing, the court can order the enforcement of the garnishment.

However, most debtors do not have valid claims for exemptions and do not file these forms. Debtors can claim exemptions here in the same way they can in the wage garnishment situation. If no exemptions are claimed within the stated time period, you can ask the court clerk to order the bank to release the money. The bank sends the money to the court, which then disburses the funds to you.

You may have noticed that the wage garnishment is called a *Writ of Continuing Garnishment* while the bank garnishment is just a *Writ of Garnishment....* This is because, while the garnishment on earnings is in effect for 90 days, the bank garnishment is a one-time enforcement tool. The bank will

NOTICE TO JUDGMENT DEBTOR OF EXEMPTION AND PENDING LEVY

This Writ with Notice is a court order which may cause your property or money to be held and taken to pay a judgment entered against you. You have legal rights which may prevent all or part of your money or property from being taken. That part of the money or property which may not be taken is called "exempt property." A partial list of "exempt property" is shown below, along with the law which may make all or part of your money or property exempt. The purpose of this notice is to tell you about these rights.

PARTIAL LIST OF EXEMPT PROPERTY (Numbered Statutory References are Subject to Change)

1. All or part of your property listed in Sections 13-54-101 and 102, C.R.S., including clothing, jewelry, books, burial sites, household goods, food and fuel, farm animals, seeds, tools, equipment and implements, military allowances, stock-in-trade and certain items used in your occupation, bicycles, motor vehicles (greater for disabled persons), life insurance, income tax refunds, money received because of loss of property or for personal injury, equipment that you need because of your health, or money received because you were a victim of a crime.
2. All or part of your earnings under Section 13-54-104, C.R.S.
3. Worker's compensation benefits under Section 8-42-124, C.R.S.
4. Unemployment compensation benefits under Section 8-80-103, C.R.S.
5. Group life insurance benefits under Section 10-7-205, C.R.S.
6. Health insurance benefits under Section 10-16-212, C.R.S.
7. Fraternal society benefits under Section 10-14-403, C.R.S.
8. Family allowances under Section 15-11-404, C.R.S.
9. Teachers' retirement fund benefits under Section 22-64-120, C.R.S.
10. Public employees' retirement benefits (PERA) under Sections 24-51-212 and 24-54-111, C.R.S.
11. Social security benefits (OASDI, SSI) under 42 U.S.C. 407
12. Railroad employee retirement benefits under 45 U.S.C. 231m.
13. Public assistance benefits (such as OAP, AFDC, TANF, AND, AB, LEAP) under Section 26-2-131, C.R.S.
14. Policemen's and firemen's pension fund payments under Sections 31-30-1117, 31-30.5-208, 31-31-203, C.R.S.
15. Utility and security deposits under Section 13-54-102(1)(r), C.R.S.
16. Proceeds of the sale of homestead property under Section 38-41-207, C.R.S.
17. Veteran's Administration benefits under 38 U.S.C. 5301
18. Civil service retirement benefits under 5 U.S.C. 8346
19. Mobile homes and trailers under Section 38-41-201.6, C.R.S.
20. Certain retirement and pension funds and benefits under Section 13-54-102(s), C.R.S.

If the money or property which is being withheld from you includes any "exempt property," you must file within 10 days of receiving this notice a written Claim of Exemption with the Clerk of the Court describing what money or property you think is "exempt property" and the reason that it is exempt. YOU MUST USE THE APPROVED FORM attached to this Writ or a copy of it. When you file the claim, you must immediately deliver, by certified mail, return receipt requested, a copy of your claim to the Garnishee (person/place that was garnished) and to the Judgment Creditor's attorney, or if none, to the Judgment Creditor at the address shown on this Writ with Notice. Notwithstanding your right to claim the property as "exempt", no exemption other than the exemptions set forth in Section 13-54-104(3), C.R.S., may be claimed for a Writ which is the result of a judgment taken for arrearages for child support or for child support debt.

Once you have properly filed your claim, the court will schedule a hearing within 10 days. The Clerk of the Court will notify you and the Judgment Creditor or attorney of the date and time of the hearing, by telephone, by mail or in person.

When you come to your hearing, you should be ready to explain why you believe your money or property is "exempt property". If you do not appear at the scheduled time, your money or property may be taken by the Court to pay the judgment entered against you.

REMEMBER THAT THIS IS ONLY A PARTIAL LIST OF "EXEMPT PROPERTY"; you may wish to consult with a lawyer who can advise you of your rights. If you cannot afford one, there are listings of legal assistance and legal aid offices in the yellow pages of the telephone book.

You must act quickly to protect your rights. Remember, you only have 10 days after receiving this notice to file your claim of exemption with the Clerk of the Court.

RETURN OF SERVICE

STATE OF COLORADO   _____ County of _____

I, _____ , affirm that I served a copy of this Writ of Garnishment
on _____ (date), at _____ (time), by _____
_____ .

Subscribed under oath before me on _____
                                Date   Signature

_____   My Commission Expires: _____   Service Fee $ _____
Notary Public

No. 1143. (Page 3 of 3)

(C.R.C.P. 30)

☐ County Court ☐ District Court _____ County, Colorado Court address:	
Petitioner(s)/Plaintiff(s): v. **Respondent(s)/Defendant(s):**	
Judgment Debtor's Attorney or Judgment Debtor (Name and Address):	
	▲ COURT USE ONLY ▲
	Case Number:
Phone Number: E-mail:	
Fax Number: Atty. Reg. #:	Division: Courtroom:

CLAIM OF EXEMPTION TO WRIT OF GARNISHMENT WITH NOTICE

NOTICE TO JUDGMENT DEBTOR:
THIS FORM MUST BE USED TO CLAIM YOUR PROPERTY IS EXEMPT FROM GARNISHMENT

My Name _____ Phone _____

Address _____
(Street, City, State, Zip Code)

I BELIEVE THE FOLLOWING PROPERTY IS EXEMPT:

Description of Property Being Held:
_____
_____

Value of Property Being Held: $ _____

Amount of Value I Claim is Exempt: $ _____

I Claim the Property is Exempt Because (Please write the Exemption(s) listed in the Writ of Garnishment With Notice, if applicable)_____
_____
_____

I certify I mailed a copy of this document by certified mail, return receipt requested, to:

THE PERSON/PLACE THAT WAS GARNISHED   JUDGMENT CREDITOR OR ATTORNEY

Address: _____   Address:_____

_____CO. _____   _____CO. _____

Subscribed under oath on _____   _____
                           Date   Signature of Judgment Debtor

_____
Notary Public/Deputy Clerk

My Commission Expires: _____

No. 1144. Rev. 8-01. **CLAIM OF EXEMPTION TO WRIT OF GARNISHMENT WITH NOTICE**

Bradford Publishing, 1743 Wazee St., Denver, CO 80202 — (303) 292-2500 — www.bradfordpublishing.com

examine the debtor's accounts to see what amounts are in them on the day it processes the garnishment, and reply accordingly. If the debtor makes a large deposit in the same account a week later, you cannot intercept the money because your garnishment does not continue to be in effect. You are allowed, however, to serve another garnishment on the same bank if you have reason to expect that this has happened. The usual scenario, though, is that the debtor will go to great lengths to avoid putting any more money in an account he knows you know about.

Bank garnishments can also work against joint accounts. You cannot go after assets which are listed solely in the name of the debtor's spouse but you can garnish funds in a joint account as long as the debtor is listed on the account. If the debtor has access to the funds in the joint account, you can garnish all the money in that account.

GARNISHING THE BANK ACCOUNT OF A BUSINESS

You can also garnish the bank accounts of businesses, partnerships, associations, and corporations. There is a separate form No. 1146, *Writ of Garnishment – Judgment Debtor Other Than a Natural Person,* for this procedure. This form can also be obtained from Bradford Publishing in Denver, local office supply stores which carry forms and sometimes from the court. The rules are basically the same as when you garnish the bank account of a real person. Complete the form, file it with the court, serve it on the bank, and await the bank's answer. If the bank is in the possession of money that belongs to the debtor entity, you can proceed as you would against an individual debtor.

The bank garnishment can be a very effective tool to collect from a debtor who appears to have no steady job or other source of income, as well as from debtors who appear to have both. Doing some detective work up front by gathering the locations and numbers of the debtor's bank accounts can often result in big collections.

(C.R.C.P. 32)

☐ County Court　　☐ District Court _____ County, Colorado Court address: **Plaintiff(s)/Petitioner(s):** v. **Defendant(s)/Respondent(s):** Judgment Creditor's Attorney or Judgment Creditor (Name and Address): Phone Number:　　　　　　　　E-mail: FAX Number:　　　　　　Atty. Reg. #:	 ▲　COURT USE ONLY　▲ Case Number: Division:　　　Courtroom:

WRIT OF GARNISHMENT–JUDGMENT DEBTOR OTHER THAN NATURAL PERSON

Judgment Debtor's name, last known address, other identifying information: _____
_____

1. Original Amount of Judgment Entered _____ $ _____
2. Plus any Interest Due on Judgment (____ % per annum) ⁽ᵈᵃᵗᵉ⁾ + $ _____
3. Taxable Costs (including estimated cost of service of this Writ) + $ _____
4. Less any Amount Paid – $ _____
5. Principal Balance/Total Amount Due and Owing = $ _____

I affirm that I am authorized to act for the Judgment Creditor and this is a correct statement as of_____.
　　　　　　　　　　　　　　　　　　　　　　　　　　　　　　　　　　　　(date)

Subscribed under oath before me on _____

_____
Notary Public or Deputy Clerk

My Commission Expires: _____

_____
(Print Judgment Creditor's Name)

Address: _____

By: _____
　　　Signature (Type Name, Title, Address and Phone)

WRIT OF GARNISHMENT

THE PEOPLE OF THE STATE OF COLORADO to the Sheriff of any Colorado County, or to any person over the age of 18 years who is not a party to this action:

You are directed to serve a copy of this Writ of Garnishment upon_____
_____, Garnishee, with proper return of service to be made to the Court.

TO THE GARNISHEE:

YOU ARE HEREBY SUMMONED AS GARNISHEE IN THIS ACTION AND ORDERED:

　a.　To answer the following questions under oath and file your answers with the Clerk of the Court (AND to mail a completed copy with your answers to the Judgment Creditor or attorney when a stamped envelope is attached) within 10 days following service of this Writ upon you. **YOUR FAILURE TO ANSWER THIS WRIT MAY RESULT IN THE ENTRY OF A DEFAULT AGAINST YOU.**

　b.　To hold pending court order any personal property owed to or owned by the Judgment Debtor and in your possession or control on the date and time this Writ was served upon you.

(See Reverse Side)

LIENS AGAINST REAL ESTATE

Another asset which you may target in your collection effort is the debtor's real property. This route generally does not result in quick collection of your claim, but it can make the debtor uncomfortable and, in some circumstances, will compel him to settle his debt with you.

When you have determined from your calls to the county assessor's office where a debtor owns real estate, you can begin the process of placing a lien on that property. The property can be located in any county in Colorado, regardless of where the debtor lives, works, or does business. The rules regarding venue do not apply to liens on real estate.

The first step is to ask a clerk in the court where you got your judgment for a *Transcript of Judgment* from your case. This document will cost you about $10. Take this *Transcript of Judgment* to the clerk and recorder—not the clerk of the court—of the county where the real estate is located. Ask the clerk and recorder to record your *Transcript of Judgment* in that county. You will again be assessed a small fee. Your recorded judgment entitles you to a lien on any property the debtor owns in that county for the next six years. This includes any property the debtor may later acquire in that county.

The lien is good for six years from the date of the entry of the judgment, not from the date of the filing of the lien. If necessary, you can renew your lien in that county by requesting that the clerk and recorder "revive" your lien prior to the date of its expiration. You can record liens in as many Colorado counties as the debtor has property.

After you have recorded a lien, you should notify the debtor that you have taken this action. This can be done with a letter sent regular mail with a copy of any relevant paperwork included. The practical effect of filing a lien on real property is that the debtor will not be able to sell the property or refinance a loan on it until the lien is removed as a result of paying off your judgment. If the debtor wants to sell the property or refinance his mortgage, he will have to settle with you. You can then release the lien by using a standard form No. 220, *Release of Lien*, available from Bradford Publishing Company in Denver or stores that sell legal forms. If, however, the debtor never tries to sell or refinance, your lien will probably not result in a collection.

WRITS OF EXECUTION

Writs of execution are used to seize the real and personal property of debtors so that the property can be sold to pay off the debtor's creditors. They can allow you to seize property such as cars, boats, even houses, and also to enter the home or place of business of the debtor to take items to satisfy the debt.

A note of warning is necessary here. While it may sound good to go in and clear out the debtor's house to pay your claim, keep in mind that this is a very radical enforcement remedy. It is extremely complicated, even for many attorneys. Many rules, procedures, and timeframes must be adhered to exactly to seize the debtor's property successfully. You will have to incur more than the usual amount of up front costs, which you may never recover. If you truly wish to proceed with this option, it is strongly recommended that you do so with the assistance of an attorney familiar with this area of the law.

Let's examine the situation in which your debtor drives a brand-new Ford Explorer. You noticed that he even had the gall to drive it to the court hearing. Why, you wonder, can't this person pay the measly $1,500 he owes me when he drives a new car? There are several possibilities you should consider before trying to seize this person's car. The debtor may be leasing the car, which means he does not own it and you cannot seize it. Maybe it belongs to someone else. Or the debtor owns the car, but it still has a huge loan on it. The loan might even be for more than the value of the car, leaving the debtor with no equity in the vehicle. The bank's share of the proceeds from the sale of the car would wipe out any chance you have to collect your money. Remember, the bank would be first in the line of creditors in such a case.

Now let's say the debtor drives an older car which has no loan on it, so the debtor really does own it. In this case, the debtor is allowed an exemption of $1,500 from the proceeds of the sale of the car if he uses it to get to work. The total worth of the vehicle is exempted if the debtor is disabled and uses the vehicle to drive to a place where he gets medical care or medicine. So, if the car was worth $3,500, and the debtor was not disabled, you could realize $2,000 from its forced sale. Not bad, but you need to include the large amounts of money you will spend to complete the execution in this equation.

You will have to obtain a Writ of Execution from the court for $5. You will have to pay the sheriff to seize the car, which will cost $50 or so. You will also need to hire a tow truck to move the car for, say, $75. The car must then be towed to a secure place, which often means a yard supervised by the towing company. Charges here can run about $10 a day. You will have to pay these storage charges for at least a month, and pay for a newspaper advertisement announcing the sheriff's sale of the car. So far you're out about $500.

Only those people seeking bargains will see the ad and appear at the sheriff's sale. They will probably not be willing to pay the retail or book price of the car. Why should they, when there is no warranty or other guarantee offered with the car. The upshot is that the sheriff will most likely sell the car for considerably less than its fair market value. So your $2,000 is reduced by not only the costs you must put into the execution, but also by the amount under its actual value the car is finally sold for. Your net total is now not so attractive. We have not even considered other complications, such as other liens, redemption rights, and other factors which can further reduce the proceeds.

There are instances in which executing on a debtor's property makes sense. However, you may want to consult with an attorney or private collection agency before proceeding.

PRIVATE COLLECTION FIRMS

The rules of Small Claims Court do not allow you to be represented by an attorney during the actual court proceedings. However, once you obtain a judgment, you are perfectly free to seek the assistance of an attorney or others who specialize in debt collection.

There are both private law firms which specialize in debt collection, and law firms who devote much of their attorneys' practice to this area. These lawyers can be found in the yellow pages under the "Collections" section of the attorneys listing. Other debt collectors may be found under the "Collection Agencies" heading. There are in excess of one hundred such agencies and law firms listed in the Denver yellow pages.

Private collection agencies can assist you by helping with some of the collection methods described in this chapter, as well as with letters and phone calls. You will be spared the trouble and grief of trying to collect. Also, experienced agencies know just what can and cannot be done to collect your debt. They are knowledgeable about the rules governing debt collection practices.

Private agencies may charge you one of two ways. The first is to assess you a flat rate for the collection efforts. You will pay this fee even if you do not actually receive any money. Many firms also work on a contingent basis, meaning they will charge you a fee based on a percentage of the amount they collect. You will only pay this fee if a collection is made, meaning that the agency has a strong incentive to come through for you. However, these fees can range from twenty-five to fifty percent of the collected amount.

Many law firms also offer debt collection services. Typically their approach relies less on phone calls and letters and more on legal remedies. They can also advise you when you are considering filing a small claims case. As with a collection agency, a law firm can assist you in the location of a debtor's assets. Unlike a collection agency, they can represent you in any necessary litigation.

Law firms can also charge you fees in two ways. They can assess you a fee based on their attorney's hourly rate, which you will have to pay regardless of the result. Law firms also charge contingent fees, which are usually around thirty-three percent. Again, these fees are assessed only if a collection is made on your behalf.

As with any other purchase of a product or service, make sure you know what you are getting into before you sign on the dotted line. Inform yourself as to the business's fees and procedures. Do not hesitate to ask questions and shop around.

SAM'S CASE

Sam had not heard from Bob for over a month. He also had not received any word that Bob intended to appeal the judgment of the Small Claims Court in their case. He rounded up his file from the case and plotted his next move.

Sam decided to try a wage garnishment first. He knew where Bob worked, and his friend Billy T. assured him that Bob was still employed by the Thornton Glass Company. He called the Secretary of State's office to see if that firm was a corporation. The person at that office confirmed that it was, and gave Sam the name and address of the company's registered agent. Sam completed the *Writ of Continuing Garnishment* form he had picked up at Bradford Publishing. He made sure to include the costs of serving the writ in line three of the garnishment form, which he estimated to be $25 After having the court in Denver formally issue the writ, he delivered three copies of the writ, a copy of the *Objection to Calculation of the Amount of Exempt Earnings* form and a sheet of the *Calculation of Exempt Earnings* form to the sheriff's office in Adams County, which is where the registered agent was located.

Ten days later, Sam received a copy of the garnishee's answers from the Thornton Glass Company. It reported that they would withhold $250 from Bob's pay every two weeks. At that rate, the debt would be paid off in five payments, or about two and a half months. Sam would not have to file another writ of garnishment because the entire amount would be paid off in less than 180 days. He crossed his fingers and waited for the checks to come in.

One check did come in. It was indeed for $250, and was from the Denver County Court. Unfortunately, the next day, Sam received a call from Billy T., who told Sam that Bob had quit his job at Thornton Glass the week before. So much for the wage garnishment, thought Sam.

☐ County Court   ☒ District Court
__Denver__ _____ County, Colorado
Court address:
     1515 Cleveland Place
     Denver, Colorado 80203

Plaintiff(s)/Petitioner(s):
     Sam Grant, d/b/a Sam's Landscape Designs
v.
Defendant(s)/Respondent(s):
     Robert Lee

Judgment Creditor's Attorney or Judgment Creditor (Name and Address):
Sam Grant
151600 W. McPherson Avenue
Golden, CO 80419

▲ COURT USE ONLY ▲
Case Number:

Phone Number: 303-555-1111   E-mail: samg@email.com
FAX Number: 303-555-6666   Atty. Reg. #: ——

Division: Courtroom:

WRIT OF CONTINUING GARNISHMENT

Judgment Debtor's name, last known address, other identifying information: __Robert Lee, 1591 So. Dahlia Street,__
__Denver, CO, phone number 303-555-3333.__

1. Original Amount of Judgment $ __1,000.00__   DATE SUIT WAS
   a. Judgment Entered __October 2, 2002__ (date)   COMMENCED:
   b. Effective Garnishment Period   (Mark Appropriate Box)
      ☐ 90 days (Judgment entered prior to August 8, 2001)   ☐ Prior to May 1, 1991
      ☒ 180 days (Judgment entered on or after August 8, 2001)   ☒ On or After May 1, 1991
2. Plus any Interest Due on Judgment (____—____ % per annum) $ __N/A__
3. Taxable Costs (including estimated cost of service of this Writ) $ __96.80__
4. Less any Amount Paid $ __00.00__
5. Principal Balance/Total Amount Due and Owing $ __1,096.80__

I affirm that I am authorized to act for the Judgment Creditor and this is a correct statement as of ____—____.
                                                                                      (Date)

Subscribed under oath before me on _____   Sam Grant
                                                        (Print Judgment Creditor's Name)
_____   Address: __15160 W. McPherson Avenue__
Notary Public or Deputy Clerk   __Golden, CO 80419__

My Commission Expires: _____   By: *Sam Grant*
                                                        Signature (Type Name, Title, Address & Phone)

WRIT OF CONTINUING GARNISHMENT
     THE PEOPLE OF THE STATE OF COLORADO to the Sheriff of any Colorado County, or to any person over the age of 18 years
who is not a party to this action:
     You are directed to serve TWO COPIES of this Writ of Continuing Garnishment upon __Ms. Mary Todd,__
__Thornton Glass Co., 9600 N. Watkins St., Thornton, CO__ _____ ,
Garnishee, with proper return of service to be made to the Court.

TO THE GARNISHEE:
YOU ARE SUMMONED AS GARNISHEE IN THIS ACTION AND ORDERED:
     a.   To answer the following questions under oath and file your answers with the Clerk of the Court and mail a completed copy with

(Continued on Reverse Side)

No. 1140. Rev. 8-01.   WRIT OF CONTINUING GARNISHMENT (C.R.C.P. Form 26) (Page 1 of 3)
          Bradford Publishing, 1743 Wazee St., Denver, CO 80202 – 303-292-2500 – www.bradfordpublishing.com

Sam next turned to a bank garnishment. From the interrogatories, Sam was able to learn where Bob banked, and he could even produce an account number. He completed the *Writ of Garnishment with Notice of Exemption and Pending Levy* form, adding in more money for the costs of serving this writ, both on the bank and on Bob. He also noted the $250 he had received from the wage garnishment on line four of this form.

Sam again went to the court and then the Denver sheriff's office. He gave the sheriff a copy of the writ for service on the bank. Then he waited.

Two weeks later, he went to the court to check on the bank's answer to his writ of garnishment. Sam was elated when he saw that the bank's answer indicated it did have some of Bob's money and that it had now been frozen. Sam immediately took another copy of the bank garnishment and a *Claim of Exemption to Writ of Garnishment with Notice* form to the familiar faces at the sheriff's office for service on Bob. Again, he waited.

The waiting ended on a Thursday when Sam opened his mailbox to discover a check from the court for exactly $880.80.

For a moment, Sam exulted in the feeling of victory. Then he realized that what he really felt was relief.

(C.R.C.P. 29)

☐ County Court   ☒ District Court

<u>Denver</u>   County, Colorado

Court Address:
     1515 Cleveland Place
     Denver, Colorado 80203

Plaintiff(s)/Petitioner(s):
     Sam Grant, d/b/a Sam's Landscape Designs

v.

Defendant(s)/Respondent(s):
     Robert Lee

Judgment Creditor's Attorney or Judgment Creditor (Name and Address):
Sam Grant
151600 W. McPherson Avenue
Golden, CO 80419

▲   COURT USE ONLY   ▲

Case Number:

Phone Number: 303-555-1111   E-mail: samg@email.com
FAX Number: 303-555-6666   Atty. Reg. #: ——

Division: Courtroom:

WRIT OF GARNISHMENT WITH NOTICE OF EXEMPTION AND PENDING LEVY

Judgment Debtor's name, last known address, other identifying information: <u>Robert Lee, 1591 So. Dahlia</u>
<u>Street, Denver, CO, Phone Number 303-555-3333, Account #1095092066.</u>

1. Original Amount of Judgment Entered <u>October 2, 2002</u> (date)	$	<u>1,000.00</u>	
2. Plus any Interest Due on Judgment (_____ % per annum)	+ $	<u>N/A</u>	
3. Taxable Costs (including estimated cost of service of this Writ)	+ $	<u>130.80</u>	
4. Less any Amount Paid	– $	<u>250.00</u>	
5. Principal Balance/Total Amount Due and Owing	= $	<u>880.80</u>	

I affirm that I am authorized to act for the Judgment Creditor and this is a correct statement as of <u>Nov. 27, 2002</u> .
                                                                          (date)

Subscribed under oath before me on _____
                                   (Date)

Print Judgment
Creditor's Name   <u>Sam Grant</u>
Address: <u>15160 W. McPherson Avenue</u>
               <u>Golden, CO 80419</u>

_____
Notary Public or Deputy Clerk

By: *Sam Grant* _____
             Signature (Type Name, Title, Address and Phone)

My Commission Expires: _____

WRIT OF GARNISHMENT WITH NOTICE OF EXEMPTION AND PENDING LEVY

     THE PEOPLE OF THE STATE OF COLORADO to the Sheriff of any Colorado County, or to any person over the age of 18 years who is not a party to this action:
     You are directed to serve a copy of this Writ of Garnishment upon <u>James Longstreet, 1st National Bank of</u> <u>Southeast Denver, 6500 E. Hampton, Denver, CO</u>, Garnishee, with proper return of service to be made to the Court.

(See Reverse Side)

SATISFACTION OF JUDGMENT

When you have received the total amount of your judgment, it is your duty to see that the court records this fact. You should file form No. 330, *Acknowledgment of Satisfaction of Judgment,* with the court acknowledging that your judgment against the debtor has been paid in full. By doing this, you avoid having to hear from the debtor later on when the debtor cannot get a loan because the court record still shows an outstanding judgment. It is best to take care of this as soon as possible after you've been paid in full. You can purchase this form at Bradford Publishing Company.

☐ County Court   ☐ District Court
_____ County, Colorado
Court address:

Plaintiff(s):

v.
Defendant(s):

▲ COURT USE ONLY ▲

Attorney or Party Without Attorney (Name and Address):

Case Number:

Division: Courtroom:

Phone Number: E-mail:
FAX Number: Atty. Reg. #:

SATISFACTION OF JUDGMENT

For and in consideration of the sum of $ _____ (amount paid), I authorize
the Clerk of the above Court to make a record of ☐ Full ☐ Partial satisfaction of this judgment.

Date of original or amended judgment: _____

Amount of original or amended judgment: $ _____

Name(s) of judgment creditor(s): _____

_____

_____

Name(s) of judgment debtor(s): _____

_____

_____

_____   _____
Signature of Judgment Creditor*   Signature of Attorney for Judgment Creditor

STATE OF COLORADO
_____ COUNTY OF _____ } ss.

The foregoing instrument was acknowledged before me this _____ day of

_____, 20_____, by _____.

Witness my hand and seal.

My commission expires _____   _____
                                                        Clerk of Court/Notary Public
*Note: Attestation by clerk of court or notary required only if Judgment Creditor is signing. This form must be filed with the court.

No. 330. Rev. 7-00. SATISFACTION OF JUDGMENT © 1983

Bradford Publishing, 1743 Wazee St., Denver, CO 80202 — 303-292-2500 — www.bradfordpublishing.com

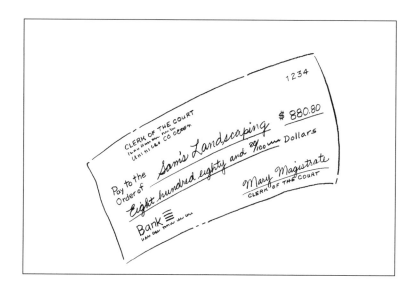

Chapter 12: Conclusion

You are now ready to take your case to Small Claims Court. You are armed with more information than most plaintiffs and defendants have when they enter that forum. The knowledge you have gained from this book has given you a clearer notion of how Small Claims Court really works. You know the rules and procedures, how to file a case, and how to collect on a judgment. Most important, you know that preparation and perseverance are key components to winning a case in Small Claims Court.

Always keep in mind that pursuing a case in Small Claims Court can be an arduous process. Litigation, even in a court with relaxed rules, is by its very nature adversarial, with each side trying to claim every advantage.

But Small Claims Court provides citizens with a unique mechanism to pursue their cases in a less threatening setting without the expense of legal representation. If you have a legitimate claim, do not be afraid to pursue it in Small Claims Court. This book provides you with the inside information and strategies you need to be successful. Thousands of others before you have prevailed in Small Claims Court. So can you.

We wish you success.

Table of Appendices

Appendix A   Glossary

Appendix B   List of forms

Appendix C   Small Claims Case Checklist

Appendix D   Small Claims Court Statutes and Rules

Appendix E   Garnishment Statutes

Appendix F   Other Statutes and Court Rules

APPENDIX A
GLOSSARY

Action – a proceeding in court in which one party seeks a remedy from another party; a lawsuit.

Answer – the legal response by the defendant to the plaintiff's claim in a complaint; the defendant's response.

Appeal – a request to a higher court for a review of the decision made by a lower court. Small claims cases are appealed to the District Court.

Certificate of Service – a signed statement which says that a legal document, such as a complaint, has been served on the appropriate person.

Colorado Revised Statutes – the laws of the State of Colorado (C.R.S.).

Complaint – the document which initiates a legal action. In Small Claims Court, this document is the "Notice, Claim, and Summons to Appear."

Creditor – the party to whom a debtor owes money; a judgment creditor.

Damages – monetary compensation which the law awards to one who has been injured by the actions of another.

Debtor – one who owes money to a creditor; a judgment debtor.

Default – a judgment entered against a party due to that party's failure to respond to another's complaint or counterclaim or to appear at trial; default judgment.

Defendant – the party being sued by the plaintiff in a legal action.

Dismissal – the end of a legal action by a court because the plaintiff has failed to appear in court or has not proved the case.

Evidence – any type of proof, such as records, documents, pictures, or the testimony of a witness, used by a party to support that party's position in a legal action.

Exhibit – a piece of physical evidence introduced at a trial.

Ex parte – a judicial proceeding is ex parte when it is held for the benefit of one party without notice to the other party. Ex parte hearings are held in Small Claims Court only when the plaintiff in a case involving restrictive covenants on residential real estate asks the court to enter temporary orders against the defendant.

File – to initiate a legal action.

Garnishee – person upon whom the judgment creditor has served a Writ of Garnishment because that person holds assets due the judgment debtor. The garnishee in a wage garnishment is typically an employer, while in a bank garnishment, the garnishee is the bank.

Garnishment – the legal process in which money in the control of a third person which is due a judgment debtor is sought by the judgment creditor. The third person can be compelled to pay a portion of the judgment debtor's money to the judgment creditor.

Hearing – a proceeding in court in which evidence is presented to the court, which then rules on the matter. In Small Claims Court, the hearing is also referred to as the trial.

Interrogatories – written questions which must be answered under oath in writing. Interrogatories in Small Claims Court can be served on defendants by plaintiffs after the court issues a ruling in favor of the plaintiff. They are used as a tool to facilitate the collection of the plaintiff's claim.

Judgment – the decision of the court in a legal action.

Judgment Creditor – the party to whom a debtor owes money in a garnishment.

Judgment Debtor – the party who owes money to a creditor in a garnishment.

Liability – responsibility for one's conduct. In Small Claims Court, liability often means a party's obligation to compensate another party for a financial injury.

Lien – a claim upon the property of another as security for a debt.

Magistrate – In Colorado, a judicial officer with many of the same powers as a judge. Many Small Claims Courts are presided over by a magistrate.

Personal Service – the delivery of a legal document to the appropriate person.

Plaintiff – the party who initiates a legal action.

Pro se – (pronounced 'pro say') – representing one's self in court without a lawyer.

Process Server – one who serves legal documents. In Colorado, this can be a sheriff, a paid private firm or individual, or any adult who is not a party to the action.

Registered Agent – the person designated by a corporation to receive legal documents. Registered agents are listed with the Colorado Secretary of State.

Response – the legal answer by the defendant to the plaintiff's claim in a complaint; the defendant's answer.

Restrictive Covenants – agreements which bind purchasers and owners of residential real property.

Service of Process – the delivery of legal documents to the appropriate person.

Statute of Limitations – law which fixes the time within which parties must take legal action to enforce rights or else be barred from enforcing them after that time has passed.

Subpoena – a document issued by a court to compel the appearance of a witness at a judicial proceeding.

Subpoena to Produce – type of subpoena issued by a court at the request of one of the parties to a legal action which requires a witness who possesses or controls certain documents or papers relevant to the case to bring these items to court during the trial. Also called a Subpoena Duces Tecum, which is Latin for "under penalty you shall take it with you."

Summons – a legal document which directs a defendant to appear in court at a time and date certain or face a judgment against the defendant for failure to do so.

Testimony – information given under oath at a trial by a witness.

Traverse – a denial by one party of another's allegations of fact. Often used in small claims actions when a garnishee replies untruthfully that he or she holds no assets of the judgment debtor because, for example, the debtor no longer is employed by the garnishee. The judgment creditor files a traverse with the court to refute the garnishee's statement.

Treble Damages – triple damages, which are available in certain limited situations under Colorado law. Treble damages are intended to punish certain types of behavior.

Trial – a proceeding in court during which evidence is presented to the court, which then rules on the matter. In Small Claims Court, the trial is also referred to as the hearing.

Venue – the place for the trial of a legal action.

Verdict – the decision of the court rendered by the judge or magistrate.

Witness – person who gives information under oath in court regarding a legal action.

APPENDIX B

These forms are used for a Small Claims Court procedure and are available free from the clerk of the court.

JDF Form No.	Title
250	NOTICE, CLAIM & SUMMONS TO APPEAR FOR TRIAL
251	NOTICE OF REMOVAL
252A	MOTION & ORDER FOR INTERROGATORIES —SHORT FORM
252B	MOTION & ORDER FOR INTERROGATORIES —LONG FORM
253	REQUEST TO SET ASIDE DISMISSAL/ DEFAULT JUDGMENT
254	SUBPOENA OR SUBPOENA TO PRODUCE
255	NOTICE OF NO SERVICE
256	NOTICE OF REPRESENTATION BY ATTORNEY
258	TEMPORARY ORDER & CITATION ENFORCEMENT OF RESTRICTIVE COVENANT ON RESIDENTIAL PROPERTY
259	OBJECTION TO MAGISTRATE HEARING CASE
260	PERMANENT ORDER

These forms are used for collection and satisfaction of your judgment and are available at Bradford Publishing Company, 1743 Wazee Street, Denver, Colorado 80202. They can be ordered by phone with a Master Card or Visa by calling (303) 292-2590.

Form No.	Title
1140	WRIT OF CONTINUING GARNISHMENT
1141	CALCULATION OF THE AMOUNT OF EXEMPT EARNINGS
1142	OBJECTION TO CALCULATION OF THE AMOUNT OF EXEMPT EARNINGS
1143	WRIT OF GARNISHMENT WITH NOTICE OF EXEMPTION AND PENDING LEVY
1144	CLAIM OF EXEMPTION TO WRIT OF GARNISHMENT WITH NOTICE
1146	WRIT OF GARNISHMENT – JUDGMENT DEBTOR OTHER THAN NATURAL PERSON
220	RELEASE OF LIEN
330	SATISFACTION OF JUDGMENT (ACKNOWLEDGMENT)
348A	RELEASE AND SETTLEMENT OF CLAIM

APPENDIX C
SMALL CLAIMS CASE CHECKLIST

Before filing a case:
- ☐ Determine if you have suffered a financial loss
- ☐ Another party is liable
- ☐ Case is appropriate for Small Claims Court
- ☐ Amount of damage is $7,500.00 or less
- ☐ Venue is proper because the other party...
  - ☐ resides in Colorado
  - ☐ is employed in Colorado
  - ☐ has an office for the transaction of business in Colorado
  - ☐ is a student at a Colorado institution of higher education
  - ☐ owns or rents property that is subject of dispute

Filing your case:
- ☐ Send the other party a demand letter
- ☐ Determine which county is best for small claims case
- ☐ Determine correct name, address, and telephone number of other party or parties
- ☐ If you are suing a corporation, obtain name and address of the corporation's registered agent
- ☐ State your claim clearly and concisely
- ☐ Complete *Notice, Claims, and Summons to Appear for Trial* form and file with court
- ☐ Serve complaint on other party via certified mail or personal service
- ☐ Check court for response by other party
- ☐ Check court to see if other party requests to transfer case to County Court.

Preparation for court:
- ☐ Review case and prepare case outline
- ☐ Gather all relevant:
  - ☐ physical evidence
  - ☐ written evidence
  - ☐ pictures and diagrams
- ☐ Prepare witnesses
- ☐ Observe other small claims hearings
- ☐ Practice presentation

- [ ] Know where courtroom is located
- [ ] Know where to park near courthouse
- [ ] Be confident, relaxed, and focused

Collecting on your judgment:
- [ ] The judgment debtor has completed interrogatories

Wage garnishment:
- [ ] Determine where judgment debtor is employed
- [ ] Determine who to serve, e.g. registered agent, business owner
- [ ] Complete *Writ of Continuing Garnishment* and file with the court
- [ ] Serve writ, *Objection to Calculation of Amount of Exempt Earnings,* and exempt earnings calculation worksheet on employer
- [ ] Check with court to see if objection has been filed by judgment debtor
- [ ] Check with court to see if garnishee has answered
- [ ] File new writ at end of 90 days if total judgment has not been paid

Bank garnishment:
- [ ] Determine at what banks judgment debtor has accounts
- [ ] Determine which branch to serve, if appropriate
- [ ] Complete *Writ of Garnishment with Notice of Exemption and Pending Levy or Writ of Garnishment – Judgment Debtor Other Than Natural Person* and file with court.
- [ ] Serve writ on bank
- [ ] Check bank's response
- [ ] If bank is holding judgment debtor's assets, serve copy of writ and *Claim of Exemption to Writ of Garnishment With Notice* on judgment debtor.
- [ ] If no objection is filed, request that court order bank to release judgment debtor's money

Lien on Real Property:
- [ ] Determine where judgment debtor owns real estate
- [ ] Obtain *Transcript of Judgment*
- [ ] File transcript with clerk and recorder in county where real estate is located
- [ ] Write to judgment debtor to inform him or her that you now have a lien on that piece of real estate

APPENDIX D
Colorado Revised Statutes

COUNTY COURT – SMALL CLAIMS DIVISION

13-6-401. Legislative declaration. The general assembly hereby finds and declares that individuals, partnerships, corporations, and associations frequently do not pursue meritorious small civil claims because of the disproportion between the expense and time of counsel and litigation and the amount of money or property involved; that the law and procedures of civil litigation are technical and frequently unknown to persons who are representing themselves; that procedures for the inexpensive, speedy, and informal resolution of small claims in a forum where the rules of substantive law apply, but the rules of procedure and pleading and the technical rules of evidence do not apply, are desirable; that such procedures should be conducted at times convenient to the persons using them, including evening and Saturday sessions; that the personnel implementing and conducting such procedures should be trained and equipped to assist anyone with a small claim in a friendly, efficient, and courteous manner; and that, therefore, the establishment of a small claims division of the county court as provided in this part 4 is in the public interest.

13-6-402. Establishment of small claims division. There is hereby established in each county court a division designated as the small claims court.

13-6-403. Jurisdiction of small claims court – limitations. (1) On and after January 1, 1996, the small claims court shall have concurrent original jurisdiction with the county and district courts in all civil actions in which the debt, damage, or value of the personal property claimed by either the plaintiff or the defendant, exclusive of interest and cost, does not exceed seven thousand five hundred dollars, including such civil penalties as may be provided by law. By way of further example, and not limitation, the small claims court shall have jurisdiction to hear and determine actions in tort and assess damages therein not to exceed seven thousand five hundred dollars. The small claims court division shall also have concurrent original jurisdiction with the county and district courts in actions where a party seeks to enforce a restrictive covenant on residential property and the amount required to comply with the covenant does not exceed seven thousand five hundred dollars, exclusive of interest and costs, in actions where a party seeks replevin if the value of the property sought does not exceed seven thousand five hundred dollars, and in actions where a party seeks to enforce a contract by specific performance or to disaffirm, avoid, or rescind a contract and the amount at issue does not exceed seven thousand five hundred dollars.

(2) The small claims court shall have no jurisdiction except that specifically conferred upon it by law. In particular, it shall have no jurisdiction over the following matters:

(a) Those matters excluded from county court jurisdiction under section 13-6-105 (1);

(b) Actions involving claims of defamation by libel or slander;

(c) Actions of forcible entry, forcible detainer, or unlawful detainer;

(d) and (e) (Deleted by amendment, L. 2001, p. 1512, § 2, effective September 1, 2001.)

(f) Actions brought or defended on behalf of a class;

(g) Actions requesting or involving prejudgment remedies;

(h) Actions involving injunctive relief, except as required to:

(I) Enforce restrictive covenants on residential property;

(II) Enforce the provisions of article 2.5 of title 6, C.R.S.;

(III) Accomplish replevin; and

(IV) Enter judgments in actions where a party seeks to enforce a contract by specific performance or to disaffirm, avoid, or rescind a contract;

(i) Traffic violations and other criminal matters;

(j) Awards of body executions.

13-6-404. Clerk of the small claims court. The clerk of the county court or a deputy designated by said clerk shall act as the clerk of the small claims court. The clerk of the small claims court shall provide such assistance as may be requested by any person regarding the jurisdiction, operations, and procedures of the small claims court; however, the clerk shall not engage in the practice of law. All necessary forms shall be available from the clerk.

13-6-405. Magistrate in small claims court. (1) In the following circumstances, a magistrate may hear and decide claims in a small claims court:

(a) In Class A counties, as defined in section 13-6-201, magistrates for small claims may be appointed by the presiding judge.

(b) In Class B counties, as defined in section 13-6-201, magistrates for small claims may be appointed, pursuant to section 13-3-105, if approved by the chief justice.

(2) A magistrate shall be a qualified attorney-at-law admitted to practice in the state of Colorado or a nonattorney if the nonattorney is serving as a county judge pursuant to section 13-6-203.

(3) While acting as a magistrate for small claims, a magistrate shall have the same powers as a judge.

(3.5) A magistrate shall have the power to solemnize marriages pursuant to the procedures in section 14-2-109, C.R.S.

(4) If any party files a timely written objection, pursuant to rule of the supreme court, with the magistrate conducting the hearing, that party's case shall be rereferred to a judge.

13-6-406. Schedule of hearings. The small claims court shall conduct hearings at such times as the judge or magistrate may determine or as the supreme court may order.

13-6-407. Parties – representation. (1) Any natural person, corporation, partnership, association, or other organization may commence or defend an action in the small claims court, but no assignee or other person not a real party to the transaction which is the subject of the action may commence an action therein, except as a court-appointed personal representative, conservator, or guardian of the real party in interest.

(2) (a) (I) Notwithstanding the provisions of article 5 of title 12, C.R.S., in the small claims court, an individual shall represent himself or herself; a partnership shall be represented by an active general partner or an authorized full-time employee; a union shall be represented by an authorized active union member or full-time employee; a for-profit corporation shall be represented by one of its full-time officers or full-time employees; an association shall be represented by one of its active members or by a full-time employee of the association; and any other kind of organization or entity shall be represented by one of its active members or full-time employees or, in the case of a nonprofit corporation, a duly elected nonattorney officer or an employee.

(II)   It is the intent of this section that no attorney, except pro se or as an authorized full-time employee or active general partner of a partnership, an authorized active member or full-time employee of a union, a full-time officer or full-time employee of a for-profit corporation, or a full-time employee or active member of an association, which partnership, union, corporation, or association is a party, shall appear or take any part in the filing or prosecution or defense of any matter in the small claims court, except as permitted by supreme court rule.

(b)   In actions arising under part 1 of article 12 of title 38, C.R.S., including, but not limited to, actions involving claims for the recovery of a security deposit or for damage to property arising from a landlord-tenant relationship, a property manager who has received security deposits, rents, or both, or who has signed a lease agreement on behalf of the owner of the real property that is the subject of the small claims action, shall be permitted to represent the owner of the property in such action.

(3)   In any action to which the federal "Soldiers' and Sailors' Civil Relief Act of 1940", 50 App. U.S.C. sec. 521, is applicable, the court may enter a default against a defendant who is in the military without entering judgment, and the court shall appoint an attorney to represent the interests of the defendant prior to the entry of judgment against the defendant.

(4)   If an attorney appears, as permitted in subsection (2) or (3) of this section, the other party or parties in the case may be represented by counsel, if such party or parties so choose.

(5)   Nothing contained in this section is intended to limit or otherwise interfere with a party's right to assign, or to employ counsel to pursue that party's rights and remedies subsequent to the entry of judgment

by a small claims court.

(6)   Any small claims court action in which an attorney appears shall be processed and tried pursuant to the statutes and court rules governing small claims court actions.

13-6-408.   Counterclaims exceeding jurisdiction of small claims court – procedures – sanctions for improper assertion. Counterclaims exceeding the jurisdiction of the small claims court shall be removed to the county or district court of appropriate jurisdiction pursuant to rule of the supreme court. If a county or district court determines that a plaintiff who originally filed a claim in the small claims court is entitled to judgment and also that a counterclaim against the same plaintiff in the small claims action was filed solely to defeat the jurisdiction of the small claims court and was without merit, the county or district court may also award the plaintiff costs, including reasonable attorney fees, incurred in prosecuting the action in the county or district court.

13-6-409.   Trial procedure. The judge or magistrate shall conduct the trial in such manner as to do justice between the parties and shall not be bound by formal rules or statutes of procedure or pleading or the technical rules of evidence, except for rules promulgated by the supreme court controlling the conduct of proceedings in the small claims court.

13-6-410.   Appeal of a claim. A record shall be made of all small claims court proceedings, and either the plaintiff or the defendant may appeal pursuant to county court rules. Upon appeal, all provisions of law and rules concerning appeals from the county court shall apply, including right to counsel. A tape recording of the trial proceedings shall satisfy any requirements of a transcript for appeal, upon the payment of a nominal fee by the appellant.

13-6-411. Limitation on number of claims filed. (1) No plaintiff may file more than two claims per month, eighteen claims per year, in the small claims court of any county. Each claim filed in any small claims court shall contain a certification by the plaintiff that the plaintiff has not filed any more than two claims during that month and eighteen claims in that year in the small claims court of that county.

(2) The limitation imposed by subsection (1) of this section shall not apply to a state-supported institution of higher education which files claims to recover loans or other outstanding obligations due to such institution; except that no such state-supported institution of higher education shall file more than a total of thirty such claims per month in all small claims courts in Colorado.

13-6-411.5. Place of trial. (1) Except as provided in subsection (2) of this section, all actions in the small claims court shall be brought in the county in which any defendant at the time of filing of the claim resides, is regularly employed, is a student at an institution of higher education, or has an office for the transaction of business.

(2) Actions to enforce restrictive covenants and actions arising under part 1 of article 12 of title 38, C.R.S., including, but not limited to, actions involving claims for the recovery of a security deposit or for damage to property arising from a landlord-tenant relationship, may be brought in the county in which the defendant's property that is the subject of the action is situated.

(3) If a defendant appears and defends a small claims action on the merits at trial, such defendant shall be deemed to have waived any objection to the place of trial permitted under this section.

13-6-412. Notice to public. The clerk of the small claims court shall publicize in an appropriate manner the existence of the small claims court, its procedures, and its hours of operation. Such publication shall be made so as to bring the court's existence to the attention of the entire community. The state court administrator shall publish a small claims court handbook outlining the procedures of the court in layman's language.

13-6-413. Supreme court shall promulgate rules. The supreme court shall implement this part 4 by appropriate rules of procedure for the small claims court.

13-6-414. No jury trial. There shall be no right to a trial by jury in the small claims court.

13-6-415. Service of process. Every defendant shall be notified that an action has been filed against that defendant in the small claims court either by certified mail, return receipt requested, or by personal service of process, as provided by the rules of procedure for the small claims court. The clerk of the small claims court shall collect, in advance, the fee provided for in section 13-32-104 (1) (i) for each service of process attempted by certified mail.

13-6-416. Facilities. No county shall be required to furnish new facilities pursuant to this part 4.

13-6-417. Execution and proceedings subsequent to judgment. Execution and proceedings subsequent to judgment entered in the small claims division may be processed in the small claims division and shall be the same as in a civil action in the county court as provided by law.

COLORADO RULES OF PROCEDURE
FOR SMALL CLAIMS COURTS

Rule 501. Scope and Purpose

(a) **How Known and Cited.** These rules for the small claims division for the county court are additions to C.R.C.P. and shall be known and cited as the Colorado Rules of Civil Procedure, or C.R.C.P. These rules are promulgated pursuant to section 13-6-413, C.R.S.

(b) **Procedure Governed.** These rules govern the procedure in all small claims courts. They shall be liberally construed to secure the just, speedy, informal, and inexpensive determination of every small claims action.

(c) **Purpose.** Each small claims court shall provide for the expeditious resolution of all cases before it. Where practicable, at least one weekend session and at least one evening session shall be scheduled or available to be scheduled for trial in each small claims court each month.

Rule 502. Commencement of Action

(a) **How Commenced.** A small claims action is commenced by filing with the court a short statement of the plaintiff's claim setting forth the facts giving rise to the action in the manner and form provided in C.R.C.P. 506 and by paying the appropriate docket fee.

(b) **Jurisdiction.** The court shall have jurisdiction from the time the claim is filed.

(c) **Setting of the Appearance Date.** At the time the small claims action is filed, the clerk shall set an appearance for a date, time and place certain. The appearance date shall not be less than thirty days from the date of issuance of the notice of claim by the clerk.

Rule 503. Place of Action

Where Brought, Generally. All actions in the small claims court shall be brought in the county in which at the time of filing of the claim any of the defendants resides, or is regularly employed, or has an office for the transaction of business, or is a student at an institution of higher education.

Rule 504. Process

(a) **Service by Certified Mail.** Within three days after the action is filed, the clerk shall send a signed and sealed notice, pursuant to Form JDF-250 appended to these rules, to the defendant(s), by certified mail, return receipt requested to be signed by addressee only, at the address supplied or designated by the plaintiff. If the notice is delivered, the clerk shall note on the register of actions and in the file the mailing date and address, the date of delivery shown on the receipt, and the name of the person who signed the receipt. If the notice was refused, the clerk shall note the date of refusal.

(b) **When Service is Complete.** Notice shall be sufficient even if refused by the defendant and returned. Service shall be complete upon the date of delivery or refusal.

(c) **Notification by Clerk and Fees and Expenses for Service.** If the notice is returned for any reason other than refusal to accept it, or if the receipt is signed by any person other than the addressee, the clerk shall so notify the plaintiff. The clerk may then issue additional notices, at the request of the plaintiff, or the plaintiff may arrange directly for personal service upon the defendant in accordance with the provisions of C.R.C.P. 304. All fees and expenses for service of process, including the postal fees for the certified mailing by the clerk, shall be paid by the plaintiff and treated as costs of the action. Issuance of each notice shall be noted upon the register of actions or in the file.

(d) Personal Service. In lieu of the provisions of this rule for service by certified mail, the plaintiff may elect to serve the defendant by personal service pursuant to C.R.C.P. 304.

Rule 505. Pleadings and Motions

(a) Pleadings. There shall be a claim and a response which may or may not include a counterclaim. No other pleadings shall be allowed.

(b) No Motions. There shall be no motions allowed except as contemplated by these rules.

Rule 506. General Rules of Pleading

(a) Claims for Relief and Responses. Except as provided in subsection (b), claims and responses, with or without a counterclaim, in the small claims court shall be filed in the manner and form prescribed by Form JDF-250 appended to these rules with a caption that conforms with C.R.C.P. 10, and shall be signed by the party under penalty of perjury. Claims and responses, with or without a counterclaim, for an action to enforce restrictive covenants on residential property shall be filed pursuant to Form JDF-257 and shall be signed by the party under penalty of perjury.

(b) Availability of Forms; Assistance by Court Personnel. The clerk of the court shall provide such assistance as may be requested by a plaintiff or defendant regarding the forms, operations, procedures, jurisdictional limits, and functions of the small claims court; however, court personnel shall not engage in the practice of law. The clerk shall also advise parties of the availability of subpoenas to obtain witnesses and documents. All necessary and appropriate forms shall be available in the office of the clerk.

Rule 507. Responses and Defenses

Each defendant shall file a written and signed response on or before the appearance date set forth in the notice of claim. At the time of filing the response or appearing, whichever occurs first, each defendant shall pay the docket fee prescribed by law.

Rule 508. Counterclaim

(a) When Counterclaim to be Filed; Effect on Hearing Date. If at the time of the appearance date it appears that a defendant has a counterclaim within the jurisdiction of the small claims court, the court may either proceed to hear the entire case or may continue the hearing for a reasonable time, at which continued hearing the entire case shall be heard.

(b) Counterclaim Within the Jurisdiction of the Small Claims Court. If at the time the action is commenced a defendant possesses a claim against the plaintiff that: (1) is within the jurisdiction of the small claims court, exclusive of interest and costs; (2) arises out of the same transaction or event that is the subject matter of the plaintiff's claim; (3) does not require for its adjudication the joinder of third parties; and (4) is not the subject of another pending action, the defendant shall file such claim as a counterclaim in the answer or thereafter be barred from suit on the counterclaim. The defendant may also elect to file a counterclaim against the plaintiff that does not arise out of the transaction or occurrence.

(c) Counterclaim Exceeding the Jurisdiction of the Small Claims Court. If at the time the action is commenced the defendant possesses a counterclaim against the plaintiff that is not within the jurisdictional limit of the small claims court, exclusive of interest and costs, and the defendant wishes to assert the counterclaim, the defendant may:

(1) file the counterclaim in the pending small claims court action, but unless the defendant follows the procedure set forth in subsection (2) below, any judgment in the defendant's favor shall be limited to the jurisdictional limit of the small claims court, exclusive of interest and costs, and suit for the excess due the defendant over that sum will be barred thereafter; or

(2) file the counterclaim together with the answer in the pending small claims court action at least seven days before the appearance date and request in the answer that the action be transferred to the county court or district court, to be tried pursuant to the rules of civil procedure applicable to the transferee court. Upon filing the answer and counterclaim, the defendant shall tender the transferee court filing fee for a complaint. Upon compliance by the defendant with the requirements of this subsection (2), all small claims court proceedings shall be discontinued and the clerk of the small claims court shall transfer the file and fee to the appropriate transferee court.

(d) Defendant Notified if Counterclaim Exceeds Court's jurisdiction. All counterclaims asserted over the jurisdictional limit of the small claims court shall be subject to the provisions of Section 13-6-408, C.R.S., and all defendants shall be advised of those provisions on Form JDF-250 appended to these rules.

Rule 509. Parties

There shall be no intervention, addition, or substitution of parties, unless otherwise ordered by the court in the interest of justice.

Rule 510. Discovery and Subpoenas

(a) No Depositions. Depositions and discovery shall not be permitted in small claims court proceedings.

(b) Subpoenas. Subpoenas for the attendance of witnesses or the production of evidence at trial shall be issued and served pursuant to C.R.C.P. 345.

Rule 511. No Jury Trial – Use of Magistrates

(a) No Jury Trial. There is no right to a trial by jury in small claims court proceedings.

(b) Magistrates. Magistrates may hear and decide claims and shall have the same powers as a judge, except as provided by C.R.M. 5(f). A party objecting to a magistrate pursuant to Section 13-6-405(4), C.R.S., shall file the objection seven days prior to the appearance date. Cases in which an objection to a magistrate has been timely filed shall be heard and decided by a judge pursuant to the rules and procedures of the small claims court.

Rule 512. Trial on the Appearance Date

(a) Date of Trial. The trial shall be held on the appearance date unless the court grants a continuance for good cause shown. A plaintiff may request one continuance if a defendant files a counterclaim.

(b) Settlement Discussions. On the appearance date, but before trial, the court may require settlement discussions between the parties, but the court shall not participate in such discussions. If a settlement is achieved, the terms of such settlement shall be presented to the court for approval. If an approved settlement is not achieved, the trial shall be held pursuant to subsection (a) of this rule.

Rule 513. Evidence

The hearing of all cases shall be informal, the object being to dispense justice promptly and economically between the parties. Rules of evidence shall not be strictly applied; however, all constitutional and statutory privileges shall be recognized. The parties may testify and offer evidence and testimony of witnesses at the hearing.

Rule 514. Judgment

At the end of the trial, the court shall immediately state its findings and decision and direct the entry of judgment. Judgment shall be entered immediately pursuant to the provisions of C.R.C.P. 358. No written findings shall be required.

Rule 515. Default

(a) Entry at the Time of Appearance and Trial. Upon the date and at the time set for appearance and trial, if the defendant has filed no response or fails to appear and if the plaintiff proves by appropriate return that proper service was made upon the defendant as provided herein at least fifteen days prior to the appearance date, the court may enter judgment for the plaintiff for the amount due, as stated in the complaint, but in no event more than the amount requested in the plaintiff's claim, plus interest, costs, and other items provided by statute or agreement. However, before any judgment is entered pursuant to this rule, the court shall be satisfied that venue of the action is proper pursuant to C.R.C.P. 503 and may require the plaintiff to present sufficient evidence to support the plaintiff's claim.

(b) Entry at the Time of Continued Trial. Failure to appear at any other date set for trial shall be grounds for entering a default and judgment against the nonappearing party.

(c) Setting Aside a Default. For good cause shown, within a reasonable period and in any event not more than thirty days after the entry of judgment, the court may set aside an entry of default and the judgment entered thereon.

Rule 516. Costs

The prevailing party in the action in a small claims court is entitled to costs of the action and also the costs to enforce the judgment as provided by law.

Rule 517. Stay of Proceedings to Enforce Judgment

(a) No Automatic Stay. If upon rendition of a judgment payment is not made forthwith, an execution may issue immediately and proceedings may be taken for its enforcement unless the party against whom the judgment was entered requests a stay of execution and the court grants such request. Proceedings to enforce execution and other process after judgment and any fees shall be as provided by law or the Colorado Rules of County Court Civil Procedure.

(b) Stay on Motion for Relief From Judgment or Appeal. In its discretion the court may stay the commencement of any proceeding to enforce a judgment pending the disposition of a motion for relief from a judgment or order made pursuant to C.R.C.P. 515(c), or pending the filing and determination of an appeal.

Rule 518. Execution and Proceedings Subsequent to Judgment

(a) Judgment Debtor to File List of Assets and Property. Immediately following the entry of judgment, the party against whom the judgment was entered, if present in court, shall complete and file the information of judgment debtor's assets and property, pursuant to Forms JDF-252(a), JDF-252(b), and JDF-252(c) appended to these rules, where appropriate and as ordered by the court, unless the judgment debtor tenders immediate payment of the judgment or the court orders otherwise.

(b) Enforcement Procedures. (1) Execution and the proceedings subsequent to judgment shall be the same as in a civil action in the county court. (2) In addition, at any time when execution may issue on a small claims court judgment, the judgment creditor shall be entitled to an order requiring the judgment debtor to appear before the court at a specified time and place to answer concerning assets and property.

Rule 519. Post Trial Relief and Appeals

No motion for new trial shall be filed in the small claims court, whether or not an appeal is taken. Appeal procedures shall be as provided by Section 13-6-410, C.R.S., and C.R.C.P. 411.

Rule 520. Attorneys and Transfer to County Court

(a) No Attorneys. Except as authorized by Section 13-6-407, C.R.S., and this rule, no attorney shall appear on behalf of any party in the small claims court.

(b) Transfer to County Court if Attorney Representation Requested. (1) On the written request of the defendant, pursuant to Form JDF-251 appended to these rules, filed not less than seven days before the appearance date, and only upon the ground that the defendant desires and will in fact have representation by an attorney, and upon payment of the appropriate county court defendant's docket fee, the clerk of the small claims court shall transfer the action to the county court. The clerk shall immediately notify the plaintiff

of the transfer, and the notice of transfer shall advise the plaintiff of the plaintiff's right to counsel. Thereupon, the plaintiff may be represented by an attorney if the plaintiff so chooses. (2) If such request to transfer is not filed at least seven days before the date set for appearance in the small claims court, an attorney shall not appear and the matter shall not be transferred to the county court.

(c) Sanctions for Delay. If the defendant, having requested and received transfer pursuant to this rule, appears at the trial without an attorney or fails to appear at the trial, and the court finds that the defendant's request for transfer was made for the purpose of delaying the trial of the plaintiff's claim, the court may award the plaintiff any costs, including reasonable attorney fees, occasioned by the delay.

(d) Transfer by Plaintiff. The plaintiff may transfer the action to the county court if, after filing the action, the plaintiff learns that the defendant will appear by an attorney pursuant to the provisions of Section 13-6-407(3), C.R.S., and the plaintiff desires and will in fact have representation by an attorney as a consequence.

(e) Small Claims Court Rules to Apply to Transferred Cases. All actions transferred to the county court solely pursuant to this rule shall be tried pursuant to the statutes and rules of procedure governing cases filed in small claims court, except that the parties may be represented by attorneys.

Rule 521. Special Procedures to Enforce Restrictive Covenants on Residential Property

(a) The small claims division shall dismiss without prejudice any claim to enforce a restrictive covenant if it affects the title to the real property.

(b) The owners of the residential property, subject of the action, shall be joined as codefendants to the action.

(c) Upon the filing of a claim under oath (see Form JDF-257) alleging that the defendant has violated any restrictive covenant regarding residential property, where the cost to comply with such restrictive covenant is not more than $3,500.00, the clerk shall issue the notice and summons to appear. The notice shall be served pursuant to C.R.C.P. 504.

(d) The general procedures applicable to the small claims court (Rules 501 through 520, C.R.C.P.) shall apply to actions to enforce a restrictive covenant on residential property, except as they are modified by this Rule.

(e) On the date set for appearance and trial pursuant to C.R.C.P. 512, the court shall proceed to determine the issues and render judgment and enter appropriate orders according to the law and the facts operative in the case.

(f) If the defendant fails to appear at the appearance date or any date to which the matter is continued, the court may proceed pursuant to C.R.C.P. 514 and the provisions of this Rule, except that the court shall require the plaintiff to present sufficient evidence to support the plaintiff's claim.

(g) An order enforcing a restrictive covenant on residential property shall be reduced to writing by the magistrate and shall be personally served upon every party subject to the order (see Form JDF-258B). If any party subject to the order is present in the courtroom at the time the order is made, the magistrate or judge shall at that time serve a copy of the order on such party and shall note such service on the order or file. Any party subject to the order who is not present shall be served as provided

by C.R.C.P. 345, except that no fees or mileage need be tendered.

(h) If the plaintiff requests a temporary order directing the defendant to immediately comply with the restrictive covenant before the defendant has had an opportunity to be heard, the plaintiff shall attach to plaintiff's complaint a certified copy of the current deed showing ownership of the residential property, and a certified copy of the restrictive covenant. The request for temporary order shall be heard by the court, ex parte, at the earliest time the court is available. If the court is satisfied from the claim filed and the testimony of the plaintiff, that there is a substantial likelihood that the plaintiff will prevail at a trial on the merits of the claim and that irreparable damage will accrue to the plaintiff unless a temporary order is issued without notice, the court may issue a temporary order and citation to the defendant to appear and show cause, at a date and time certain, why the temporary order should not be made permanent (see Form JDF-258A).

(1) A copy of the claim and notice with the attachments and with a copy of the temporary order and citation shall be served on the defendant as provided by C.R.C.P. 504, and the citation shall inform the defendant that if the defendant fails to appear in court in accordance with the terms of the citation, the restraining order may be made permanent.

(2) On the appearance date or any date to which the matter has been continued, the court shall proceed as provided in subsections (e) and (g) of this Rule.

(i) A temporary order shall not be an appealable order. A permanent order shall be an appealable order.

(j) When it appears to the court by motion supported by affidavit that a violation of the temporary or permanent order issued pursuant to this

Rule has occurred, the court shall immediately order the clerk to issue a citation to the defendant so charged to appear and show cause before a county judge at a time designated why the defendant should not be held in contempt for violation of the court's order. The citation shall direct the defendant to appear in the county court. Such contempt proceedings shall be governed by C.R.C.P. 407. The citation and a copy of the motion and affidavit shall be served upon the defendant in the manner required by C.R.C.P. 345. If such defendant fails to appear at the time designated in the citation, a warrant for the defendant's arrest may issue to the sheriff. The warrant shall fix the time for the production of the defendant in court. A bond set in a reasonable amount not to exceed $3,500.00 shall be stated on the face of the warrant.

Note: the $3,500.00 amount shown in (c) and (j) is being changed by the court to $7,500.00 to be consistent with Section 13-6-403, C.R.S.

APPENDIX E
Colorado Revised Statutes

ARTICLE 54.5
Garnishment

13-54.5-101. Definitions. As used in this article, unless the context otherwise requires:

(1) "Continuing garnishment" means any procedure for withholding the earnings of a judgment debtor for successive pay periods for payment of a judgment debt.

(2) (a) "Earnings" means:

(I) Compensation paid or payable for personal services, whether denominated as wages, salary, commission, or bonus;

(II) Funds held in or payable from any health, accident, or disability insurance.

(b) For the purposes of writs of garnishment that are the result of a judgment taken for arrearages for child support or for child support debt, "earnings" also means:

(I) Workers' compensation benefits;

(II) Any pension or retirement benefits or payments, including but not limited to those paid pursuant to article 64 of title 22, C.R.S., articles 51, 54, 54.5, 54.6, and 54.7 of title 24, C.R.S., and article 30 of title 31, C.R.S.;

(III) Payment to an independent contractor for labor or services, dividends, severance pay, royalties, monetary gifts, monetary prizes, excluding lottery winnings not required by the rules of the Colorado lottery commission to be paid only at the lottery office, taxable distributions from general partnerships, limited partnerships, closely held corporations, or limited liability companies, interest, trust income, annuities, capital gains, or rents;

(IV) Any funds held in or payable from any health, accident, disability, or casualty insurance to the extent that such insurance replaces wages or provides income in lieu of wages; and

(V) Tips declared by the individual for purposes of reporting to the federal internal revenue service or tips imputed to bring the employee's gross earnings to the minimum wage for the number of hours worked, whichever is greater.

(c) For the purposes of writs of garnishment issued by the state agency responsible for administering the state medical assistance program, which writs are issued as a result of a judgment for medical support for child support or for medical support debt, "earnings" includes:

(I) Payments received from a third party to cover the health care cost of the child but which payments have not been applied to cover the child's health care costs; and

(II) State tax refunds.

(3) "Garnishee" means a person other than a judgment creditor or judgment debtor who is in possession of earnings or property of the judgment debtor and who is subject to garnishment in accordance with the provisions of this article.

(4) "Garnishment" means any procedure through which the property or earnings of an individual in the possession or control of a garnishee are required to be withheld for payment of a judgment debt.

(5) "Judgment creditor" means any individual, corporation, partnership, or other legal entity that has recovered a money judgment against a judgment debtor in a court of competent jurisdiction.

(6) "Judgment debtor" means any person, including a corporation, partnership, or other legal entity, who has a judgment entered against him in a court of competent jurisdiction.

(7) "Notice of exemption and pending levy" means the document required to be served on the judgment debtor in any garnishment proceeding, except continuing garnishment, as soon as practicable following the service of the writ of garnishment on the garnishee. A "notice of exemption and pending levy" includes a statement that the judgment creditor intends to satisfy the judgment against the judgment debtor out of the judgment debtor's personal property held by a third party and that the judgment debtor has the right to claim certain property as exempt.

13-54.5-102. Continuing garnishment - creation of lien. (1) In addition to garnishment proceedings otherwise available under the laws of this state in any case in which a money judgment is obtained in a court of competent jurisdiction, the judgment creditor or its assignees shall be entitled, on notice to the judgment debtor required by section 13-54.5-105, to apply to the clerk of such court for garnishment against any garnishee. To the extent that the earnings are not exempt from garnishment, such garnishment shall be a lien and continuing levy upon the earnings due or to become due from the garnishee to the judgment debtor.

(2) Garnishment pursuant to subsection (1) of this section shall be a lien and continuing levy against said earnings due for one hundred eighty days following service of the writ or for one hundred eighty days following the expiration of any writs with a priority under section 13-54.5-104, but such lien shall be terminated earlier than one hundred eighty days if earnings are no longer due, the underlying judgment is vacated, modified, or satisfied in full, or the writ is dismissed; except that a continuing garnishment may be suspended for a specified period of time by the judgment creditor upon agreement with the judgment debtor, which agreement shall be in writing and filed by the judgment creditor with the clerk of the court in which the judgment was entered and a copy of which shall be delivered by the judgment creditor to the garnishee.

(3) Garnishment pursuant to subsection (1) of this section shall apply only to proceedings against the earnings of a judgment debtor who is a natural person.

13-54.5-103. Property or earnings subject to garnishment. (1) Any earnings owed by the garnishee to the judgment debtor at the time of service of the writ of continuing garnishment upon the garnishee and all earnings accruing from the garnishee to the judgment debtor from such date of service up to and including the ninetieth day thereafter shall be subject to the process of continuing garnishment. A garnishee shall not be required to collect, possess, or control the judgment debtor's tips, and any such tips shall not be owed by a garnishee to a judgment debtor.

(2) Any indebtedness, intangible personal property, or tangible personal property capable of manual delivery, other than earnings, owned by the judgment debtor and in the possession and control of the garnishee at the time of service of the writ of garnishment upon the garnishee shall be subject to the process of garnishment.

(3) Notwithstanding the provisions of subsections (1) and (2) of this section, the exemptions from garnishment required or allowed by law, including but not limited to exemptions provided by sections 13-54-102 and 13-54-104 and 15 U.S.C. sec. 1671 et seq., shall apply to all garnishments.

13-54.5-104. Priority between multiple garnishments. (1) (a) Only one writ of continuing garnishment against earnings due the judgment debtor shall be satisfied at one time. When more than one writ of continuing garnishment has been issued against earnings due the same judgment debtor, they shall be satisfied in the order of service on the garnishee. Except as provided in this subsection (1), a lien and continuing levy obtained pursuant to this article shall have priority over any subsequent garnishment lien or wage attachment.

(b) Where a continuing garnishment has been suspended for a specific period of time by agreement of the parties pursuant to the provisions of section 13-54.5-102 (2), such suspended continuing garnishment shall have priority over any writ of continuing garnishment served on the garnishee after such suspension has expired.

(c) (I) Notwithstanding any other provision of this subsection (1), a continuing garnishment obtained pursuant to section 14-14-105, C.R.S., for the satisfaction of debts or judgments for child support shall have priority over any other continuing garnishment.

(II) Notwithstanding any other provision of this subsection (1), a continuing garnishment obtained pursuant to section 26-2-128 (1) (a), C.R.S., for the satisfaction of a judgment for fraudulently obtained public assistance or fraudulently obtained overpayments has priority over any other continuing garnishment other than a garnishment for collection of child support under subparagraph (I) of this paragraph (c).

(2) (a) Any writ of continuing garnishment served upon a garnishee while any previous writ is still in effect shall be answered by the garnishee with a statement that he has been served previously with one or more writs of continuing garnishment against earnings due the judgment debtor and specifying the date on which all such liens are expected

to terminate.

(b) Upon the termination of a lien and continuing levy obtained pursuant to this article, any other writ of continuing garnishment which has been issued or which is issued subsequently against earnings due the judgment debtor shall have priority in the order of service on the garnishee, and no priority shall be given to any previous continuing lienholder whose lien has terminated. The person who serves a writ of continuing garnishment on a garnishee shall note the date and time of such service.

13-54.5-105. Notice to judgment debtor in continuing garnishment. In a case of continuing garnishment, the judgment creditor shall serve two copies of the writ of continuing garnishment upon the garnishee, one copy of which the garnishee shall deliver to the judgment debtor as provided in section 13-54.5-107. Such writ shall include notice to the judgment debtor of the formula used to calculate the amount of exempt earnings owed to the judgment debtor for a single pay period and the amount of nonexempt earnings payable to the judgment creditor for a single pay period, and such writ shall contain notice to the judgment debtor of his right to object to such calculation of exempt and nonexempt earnings and his right to a hearing on such objection.

13-54.5-107. Service of notice upon judgment debtor. (1) In a case of continuing garnishment, the garnishee shall deliver a copy of the writ of garnishment required by section 13-54.5-105 to the judgment debtor at the time the judgment debtor receives earnings for the first pay period affected by such writ of continuing garnishment.

(2) In cases where the judgment debtor's personal property, other than earnings, is subject to garnishment, service of the notice of exemp-

tion and pending levy required by section 13-54.5-106 shall be made by delivering a copy of such notice to the judgment debtor personally or by leaving a copy of such notice at the usual abode of the judgment debtor with some member of his family over the age of eighteen years. In the event that personal service cannot be made upon the judgment debtor, upon a showing that due diligence has been used to obtain personal service, the court shall order service of such notice of exemption and pending levy to be made, in accordance with section 24-70-106, C.R.S., by publication thereof for a period of ten days in some newspaper of general circulation published in the county in which said property was so levied upon or, if there is no such newspaper published in such county, by publication in a newspaper of general circulation in an adjoining county, and the court shall order the clerk of the court in which the judgment was entered to mail a copy of such notice to the judgment debtor at his last-known address, postage prepaid. Such notice, with proof of service thereof, and, in the case of publication, an affidavit of publication and an affidavit of the mailing of notice shall be filed with the clerk of the court in which the judgment was entered.

(3) Compliance with this section and sections 13-54.5-105 and 13-54.5-106 by the judgment creditor shall be deemed to give sufficient notice to the judgment debtor of the garnishment proceedings against him, and no further notice shall be required under this article.

13-54.5-108. Judgment debtor to file written objection or claim of exemption. (1) (a) In a case of continuing garnishment where the judgment debtor objects to the calculation of the amount of exempt earnings, the judgment debtor shall have five days from receipt of the copy of

the writ of continuing garnishment required by section 13-54.5-105 within which to resolve the issue of such miscalculation, by agreement with the garnishee, during which time the garnishee shall not tender any moneys to the clerk of the court. If such objection is not resolved within five days and after good faith effort, the judgment debtor may file a written objection with the clerk of the court in which the judgment was entered setting forth with reasonable detail the grounds for such objection. The judgment debtor shall, by certified mail, return receipt requested, deliver immediately a copy of such objection to the judgment creditor or his attorney of record.

(b) In a case where a garnishee, pursuant to a writ of garnishment, holds any personal property of the judgment debtor other than earnings which the judgment debtor claims to be exempt, said judgment debtor, within ten days after being served with the notice of exemption and pending levy required by section 13-54.5-106, shall make and file with the clerk of the court in which the judgment was entered a written claim of exemption setting forth with reasonable detail a description of the property claimed to be exempt, together with the grounds for such exemption. The judgment debtor shall, by certified mail, return receipt requested, deliver immediately a copy of such claim to the judgment creditor or his attorney of record.

(2) Upon the filing of a written objection or claim of exemption, all further proceedings with relation to the sale or other disposition of said property or earnings shall be stayed until the matter of such objection or claim of exemption is determined.

(3) Notwithstanding the provisions of subsection (1) of this section, a judgment debtor failing to make a written objection or claim of exemption may, at any time within six

months from receipt of a copy of the writ of continuing garnishment required by section 13-54.5-105 or from service of the notice of exemption and pending levy required by section 13-54.5-106 and for good cause shown, move the court in which the judgment was entered to hear an objection or a claim of exemption as to any earnings or property levied in garnishment, the amount of which the judgment debtor claims to have been miscalculated or which the judgment debtor claims to be exempt. Such hearing may be granted upon a showing of mistake, accident, surprise, irregularity in proceedings, newly discovered evidence, events not in the control of the judgment debtor, or such other grounds as the court may allow.

13-54.5-109. Hearing on objection or claim of exemption. (1) (a) Upon the filing of an objection pursuant to section 13-54.5-108 (1) (a) or the filing of a claim of exemption pursuant to section 13-54.5-108 (1) (b), the court in which the judgment was entered shall set a time for the hearing of such objection or claim, which shall be not more than ten calendar days after filing. The clerk of the court where such objection or claim is filed shall immediately inform the judgment creditor or his attorney of record and the judgment debtor or his attorney of record by telephone, by mail, or in person of the date set for such hearing.

(b) The certificate of the clerk of the court that service of notice of such hearing has been made in the manner and form stated in paragraph (a) of this subsection (1), which certificate has been attached to the court file, shall constitute prima facie evidence of such service, and such certificate of service filed with the clerk of the court is sufficient return of such service.

(2) Upon such hearing, the court shall summarily try and determine whether the amount of the judgment debtor's exempt earnings was correctly calculated by the garnishee or whether the property held by the garnishee is exempt and shall enter an order or judgment setting forth the determination of the court. If the amount of exempt earnings is found to have been miscalculated or if said property is found to be exempt, the court shall order the clerk of the court to remit the amount of over-garnished earnings, or the garnishee to remit such exempt property, to the judgment debtor within three business days.

(3) Where the judgment debtor moves the court to hear an objection or claim of exemption within the time provided by section 13-54.5-108 (3) and the judgment giving rise to such claim has been satisfied against property or earnings of the judgment debtor, the court shall hear and summarily try and determine whether the amount of the judgment debtor's earnings paid to the judgment creditor was correctly calculated and whether the judgment debtor's property sold in execution was exempt and shall issue an order setting forth the determination of the court. If such amount of earnings is found to have been miscalculated or if such property is found to be exempt, the court shall order the judgment creditor to remit the amount of the over-garnished earnings or such exempt property or the value thereof to the judgment debtor within three business days.

(4) Any order or judgment entered by the court as provided for in subsections (2) and (3) of this section is a final judgment or order for the purpose of appellate review.

13-54.5-110. No discharge from employment for any garnishment – general prohibition. (1) No employer shall discharge an employee for the reason that a creditor of the employee has subjected or attempted to subject unpaid earnings of the employee to any garnishment or like proceeding directed to the employer for the purpose of paying any judgment.

(2) If an employer discharges an employee in violation of the provisions of this section, the employee may, within ninety days, bring a civil action for the recovery of wages lost as a result of the violation and for an order requiring the reinstatement of the employee. Damages recoverable shall be lost wages not to exceed six weeks, costs, and reasonable attorney fees.

13-54.5-111. Supreme court rules. The practice and procedure in garnishment actions instituted pursuant to this article, and all forms in connection therewith, shall be in accordance with rules prescribed by the supreme court pursuant to article 2 of this title.

APPENDIX F

Below is a list of other Colorado Statutes and Court Rules that may be helpful in researching your case or collecting your judgment.

C.R.S. means Colorado Revised Statutes
C.R.C.P. means Colorado Rules of Civil Procedure

Attachments – Rule 402, C.R.C.P.

Bad Check Debt – Section 13-21-109, C.R.S.

Garnishment – Sections 13-54-101 through 13-54.5-111, C.R.S. and Rule 403, C.R.C.P.

Landlord/Tenant Laws – Sections 13-40-101 through 13-40-123, C.R.S.

Motor Vehicle Purchases – Sections 42-10-101 through 42-10-107, C.R.S.

Motor Vehicle Repair – Sections 42-9-101 through 42-9-112, C.R.S.

Security Deposits – Sections 38-12-101 through 38-12-104, C.R.S.

Service of Process – Rule 304, C.R.C.P.

Unpaid Wages – Sections 8-4-101 through 8-4-126, C.R.S.

Index